The Spellmount Siegfried Line Series

Vol. 1 *West Wall: The Battle for Hitler's Siegfried Line* (available)
The story of Hitler's top secret line of fortifications which turned out to
be Germany's last line of defence in the final year of World War II

Vol. 2 *'44: In Combat from Normandy to the Ardennes* (available)
Eyewitness accounts of the attack from the beachhead to the Wall

Vol. 3 *Bloody Aachen* (available)
The first major battle for the most impregnable part of the West Wall

Vol. 4 *The Battle of Hurtgen Forest* (available)
The officially covered-up defeat of 12 US Divisions;
the lead up to the Battle of the Bulge

Vol. 5 *Ardennes: The Secret War* (available)
The secret preparations for the 'surprise attack' in the Ardennes –
the US's 'Gettysburg of the 20th century'

Vol. 6 *Decision at St Vith* (available)
The decisive battle for the West Wall frontier town that broke
the back of the German assault

Vol. 7 *The Other Battle of the Bulge: Operation* Northwind (available)
The unknown battle fought by the US 7th Army –
the 'Forgotten Army' – in Alsace

Vol. 8 *Patton's Last Battle* (available)
Patton's major breakthrough in the West Wall,
before his fall from grace and his accidental death

Vol. 9 *Bounce the Rhine* (available)
The British role in breaching the West Wall,
and the triumphant crossing of the Rhine

Vol. 10 *Paths of Death and Glory*
The Last Days of the Third Reich
The battle for Europe, January – May 1945

PATHS OF DEATH AND GLORY

THE LAST DAYS OF THE THIRD REICH

by

Charles Whiting

SPELLMOUNT
Staplehurst

British Library Cataloguing in Publication Data:
A catalogue record for this book is available
from the British Library

Copyright © Charles Whiting 1997, 2003

ISBN 1-86227-210-7

First published in 1997 by
Severn House Publishers Ltd

This edition first published in the UK in 2003 by
Spellmount Limited
The Old Rectory
Staplehurst
Kent TN12 0AZ

Tel: 01580 893730
Fax: 01580 893731
E-mail: enquiries@spellmount.com
Website: www.spellmount.com

1 3 5 7 9 8 6 4 2

Printed in Great Britain by
T.J. International, Padstow, Cornwall

Contents

"The world must know that this State will, therefore, never capitulate."

Adolf Hitler, 1 January 1945.

List of Plates

a dead German civilian who attempted to shoot a British
sentry.
20. The victors. The men of The Wiltshire Regiment who have
just captured a German command post.
21. The Brussels Standard marches past.
22. The author where it all started: Stolzemburg, where US troops
first crossed into Germany, 11 September 1944.

Preface

We heard them before we saw them. The stamp of marching boots down the dusty German road and the hundreds of voices singing lustily. What they sang fifty years ago escapes me now. Perhaps it was *Oh, du schöner Westerwald* or some such harmless folksong. Now Germany was finished and they were marching into captivity; they wouldn't want to rile us, the victors. The defiant U-boat men turned infantry, we'd taken the week before, had still sung that provocative *Wir fahren gegen England** as they had been marched off to the cages. This lot knew they had lost; that there was no hope for Germany now.

"What they're singing for?" Big Slack (Arse) asked in that naïve fashion of his. "They've nowt to sing about."

"Jerries allus fooking sing," his fellow Geordie, Little Slack, answered scornfully. "Cos Jerries have nae fooking sense. That's fooking why."

"Oh ay," Big Slack said, as if his mate's answer explained everything.

At the crossroads waiting for them, "Big Tam", the major, stiffened, the ribbons of his balmoral fluttering in the breeze. Slowly he raised his hand to his bonnet in salute. Then they were there. The officers of the *Grossdeutschland Division*, coming to surrender.

They were hard, stern men, all of them. Their elegant tunics were covered in the decorations of six years of war: Iron Cross,

* We sail against England.

German Cross in Gold, Silver Wound Medal and all the rest of the "tin", as they called their medals. These were the men who Hitler had sent out to conquer Europe in 1939 and they had done so. They had been bold, brave and resourceful. Now they were beaten at last, their world shattered. Stiffly they marched past the major and the rest of us, their eyes not seeming to see us.

Behind them came the rank and file. They sang now no more. Nor did they march. Instead they shuffled along the dusty road. A lot of them were kids like we were. Some – by our standards – were very old. They could have been our grandfathers. But all of them were scruffy and shabby in long grey overcoats of cheap material which flapped about their ankles. Probably they'd be lousy, too, we thought. German prisoners usually were. Unlike their officers they were curious. They stared with interest at their captors. Some even attempted a cautious smile. They were POWs now admittedly, but at least we weren't the feared "Ivans", as they called the Russians. With us, they knew, they'd get fairly decent treatment. We were the "Tommies", who might loot their wallets and wrist-watches, but that would be about it.

So they marched by us in their hundreds on the way to the cages. Big Tam said, "Now don't let any of them slip away, chaps." When he'd gone, Little Slack said contemptuously, "Don't let 'em fooking slip away! They can all fooking sling their hook as far as I'm concerned." He tapped his fat chest, as usual covered by a dirty khaki pullover, "Me, I've seen enough fooking Jerries to last me a fooking lifetime."

We all had. All our young lives seemed to have been dominated by the "Jerries". Our fathers and grandfathers had told us about them "in the trenches". The maimed, crippled shell-shocked victims of that "Great War" had been all around us as kids. Then had come Hitler. Thereafter, every new year had brought a new crisis. Even the thickest of us had known as kids that war with Germany would be inevitable.

x

"It is the German century," our history master had pontificated at school, "at least as far as the Continent is concerned. The Germans dominate Europe militarily, economically and politically. Broadly speaking, the Germans will determine what happens to the rest of us."

I told myself on that May day that my history teacher had been proved wrong. Germany had been soundly beaten. Its cities were in ruins and Germany itself had been a battlefield for nearly six months. This time the Germans couldn't complain they had lost the war not in battle but by treachery at home, as they had done after the first war. This time they had seen their army defeated in their own country. No, it definitely wasn't to be Germany's century.

In the event, I was wrong and my history teacher right. But that is another matter. On that warm May day half a century ago, we – Americans, Britons, Canadians and soldiers of a dozen different allied nations who had taken part in the campaign – knew we had beaten the Germans.

Back in September 1944 when the Allies first reached Germany's frontiers, most commentators thought the war would be over by Christmas. That had not been the case. Many of those who reached the borders of the Reich that September did not survive into 1945 when a new and bitterly fought campaign commenced – the hard slog right across that Third Reich which Hitler had boasted would last a thousand years. Allied soldiers fought battles through Hitler's Reich from the shores of the Baltic in the north to the Brenner Pass in the south-east. Virtually every great German city, save Hamburg, had to be fought for and it was only when that evil genius, Hitler, was dead that the real mass surrenders commenced.

The cost was high. In the last six weeks alone, Montgomery lost 30,000 men and 2,000 tanks as his armies headed for the Baltic. American losses in their drive towards Italy and Austria were just as high. Almost to the very last the Germans defended their beaten country with savage ferocity. This story is about the men – and women – who fought those last battles in Europe; how they lived, how they died. It was their "blood, sweat and tears" which made victory in Europe possible. That great Tuesday, 8 May 1945, which would go down in history as VE Day.

C.W. Bleialf, Germany
York, England
Spring 1997

Acknowledgements

I am indebted to many people for assistance in preparing this book. Much of the material goes back many years when I interviewed people such as the "Last Führer", Admiral Doenitz, my old corps commander, General Horrocks, Hitler's two secretaries etc. More recent material has been provided by the old comrades of the 3rd, 45th and 70th US Infantry Divisions.

In particular, I would like to thank Tom Dickinson of New York and his old wartime buddy, Hy Schorr of the same city, and Professor Jim Thorpe of Maryland as well as Professor Hobie Morris of New York state.

C.W.

JANUARY

"We can still lose this war."

General George Patton,
4 January 1945

I

Five minutes to midnight. 31 December 1944. On that freezing Sunday night in Alsace, two young officers, Lieutenants George Bradshaw and Richard Shattuck decided that someone in the US 44th Infantry Division's Fox Company should celebrate the advent of 1945. Despite the cold and the snow, the two young and high-spirited officers clambered out of their foxholes to wait for the new year.

For nearly two days now the relatively green 44th Division had been dug in between the French industrial towns of Sarreguemines and Rimling at the extreme left of the US Seventh Army's long front in France. Tension had been rising all that time. The GIs had not been told officially that there was a "flap" on. But they knew from their contacts with local civilians and by the anxious looks on the faces of visiting staff officers that, as they phrased it in their own crude jargon, soon "the shit is gonna hit the fan". Why else should they have to stand to virtually every night? Why should they have double the normal number of men in the line? No, the men of the 44th Infantry knew instinctively that the Top Brass in the "head shed" was expecting some sort of German attack.

Unabashed by what might come, the two young officers stood in the moonlit snow. They raised their carbines ready to fire a *feu de joie* at the stroke of midnight, while in their holes the doughboys grinned at the crazy antics of the two shavetail lieutenants.

"Two minutes to go!" Bradshaw called to Shattuck. He

3

clicked off his safety catch and began to count off the seconds to 1945.

But Bradshaw was not fated to fire his salute to 1945. Suddenly, startlingly, bullets began to kick up the snow in angry spurts all around him. In that same instant, a fighter plane came howling down out of the moonlit sky. At zero feet it hurtled across the snowfield, dragging its monstrous shadow behind it. Angry purple flame rippled the length of its wings, as it proceeded to shoot up the positions of Fox Company. Then it was gone, disappearing as abruptly as it had come, soaring back to Germany.

Shakily the two young officers rose to their feet, patting the snow from their uniforms. "What the hell's going on, Dick?" Bradshaw called to his buddy. Shattuck didn't know. But already he could hear the rattle of tank tracks to their front – and the 44th Infantry Division possessed no tanks! The long-awaited German attack was coming in . . .

In Berlin Hitler was shouting shrilly into the microphone. "Our people are resolved to fight the war to victory under any and all circumstances," he declared to the listening German people. "We are going to destroy everybody who does not take part in the common effort for the country or makes himself a tool of the enemy . . . The world must know that this State will, therefore, never capitulate . . . Germany will rise like a phoenix from its ruined cities and this will go down in history as the miracle of the twentieth century!"

"I want, therefore, in this hour, as spokesman of Greater Germany to promise solemnly to the Almighty that we shall fulfil our duty faithfully and unshakeably in the New Year, in the firm belief that the hour will strike when victory will ultimately come to those most worthy of it – the Greater German Reich!"

Even as the Führer spoke, eight of his divisions were attacking the US Seventh Army in Alsace. Before dawn the

44th Infantry Division was being attacked everywhere. Its neighbour the 100th, "Century Division", had been cut off and Task Force Hudelson, linking the 100th to the US 45th Division, was breaking down under the German assault, with one of its officers signalling to his commander, "God, my men are being cut to pieces!"

For the veteran 45th Infantry Division, which had been in constant combat since it landed in Sicily in 1943, the first day of 1945 dawned bright and beautiful. Their front was still quiet. As the journal of the Division's 137th Infantry Regiment recorded, "Jan. 1, 1945 . . . clear, cold day. The type of day Americans are apt to call perfect football weather." Soon something more lethal than a football would be coming the Division's way.

Back in mid-December, the Division's morale had sunk when the Germans had launched their surprise attack in the Belgian Ardennes, soon to be known as the "Battle of the Bulge". Rumour abounded, *Normandy troops fleeing back to the beaches . . . Patton has been routed . . . tremendous new Dunkirk in the making . . .* But morale had risen again at the news that Patton's Third Army had relieved the surrounded US 101st Airborne Division at the Belgian town of Bastogne.

Now this Monday morning as new rumours came flooding in about the plight of the 44th and 100th Divisions, the veterans didn't take them so seriously. To their rear the "feather merchants" and "canteen commandos", as the frontline troops called the service and supply troops contemptuously, did. As the chronicler of the Division's 179th Regiment noted afterwards, "Rear echelons, remembering the fate of the US First Army*, all packed up and fled! Leaving food uneaten on the table, they partied** and never stopped until they had reached Luneville."

* The First Army had been caught by surprise by the German attack in the Ardennes on 16 December 1944.
** GI slang for "left", from the French verb *"partir"* – to leave.

Traffic behind the front was paralysed. The roads were jammed with trucks, jeeps, trailors and vans, all retreating. The terrible waste that always follows an army was multiplied tenfold as equipment was abandoned on every road leading to the rear. Like H.G. Wells' *End of the World*, as the 179th's chronicler wrote, "the rear pulled out as if the end *had* really come".

But now the 45th Division was being drawn into the new battle. As the plight of the Task Force became ever more apparent, the 45th's 179th Infantry Regiment was ordered to fill up the gap. The march forward was terrible. Trucks and vehicles skidded and slithered off the icy roads. They passed troops from the Rest Centre fleeing westwards. With them were those Alsatians who feared what could happen to them when the Germans came back again – frightened old women and children, dragging all their worldly goods behind them on wooden carts. As the chronicler of the 179th records: "we were passing . . . through a confusion that, on a small scale, must have resembled the French débâcle of '40".

Patrols from the advancing Germans began probing the 45th's positions everywhere. A column of German horsedrawn artillery was reported about to attack the 45th's 157th Regiment. Air support was whistled up. The weather was perfect for an aerial attack – hard, bright, blue sky. But as so often before, "the American Luftwaffe", as it was named by the hard-pressed cynical footsloggers of the infantry, missed the Germans and bombed the 45th instead.

Now the whole of the US Seventh Army was under severe pressure. More and more units were withdrawing, with or without permission. An unknown officer of the 117th Cavalry called the headquarters of the 45th and stated lamely, "we're falling back a little".

"How far is a little?" he was asked.

"About two thousand yards."

The staff officer knew how much a withdrawal of that

magnitude might affect the Division's position. Anxiously he queried, "Do you *have* to fall back that far?"

The answer was a click on the phone. The unknown cavalry-man had hung up. When next heard from the 117th Cavalry had fallen back much more than just over a mile. In fact it had retreated nine miles to the little Alsatian town of Wingen. When it got there and found the German SS in possession, it did another bunk. This time it disappeared from the combat zone completely. It was clear that the Inspector-General's branch, which looked into breaches of military discipline, would have a lot on its plate when this particular battle was over.

In the sky the Germans were on the offensive, too. On that Sunday/Monday night, the *Sylvester* night of, 1945, the thousand-odd *Luftwaffe* pilots and their crews did not celebrate, as was the German custom, with *Sekt und Bleigiessen* (champagne and the casting of molten lead to reveal the future). Instead they slept and waited for first light, which would bring the greatest air strike carried out by the *Luftwaffe* since that heady year of victories, 1940.

At five o'clock that Monday morning the air crew were served their "nigger sweat" (black coffee) and "dog biscuits" (hard tack), and if their stomachs could stand it at that time of the day "rubber eggs", i.e. scrambled eggs made from egg powder. A final briefing – there was a touch of ground fog in places – and they were airborne. A thousand German planes from ten different wings spread out in four massive formations, each wing assigned to attack specific targets behind the Allied lines.

From the Rhine to the snow-bound front in Belgium, Holland and France they were led by old-fashioned "Auntie Ju's", lumbering, antiquated three-engined Junkers 52. Most of the pilots taking part in this last great *Luftwaffe* air strike were green, straight out of the Reich's flying schools.

Down below the German flak opened up. The teenage

7

gunners had been warned to expect something unusual this freezing January morning. But as they were used to Allied domination of the sky above the Reich, they thought these planes were the usual "aerial gangsters of the RAF" returning after some raid or other on Germany's pulverised cities. Four of the attack force went down in flames, but the rest continued their steady progress westwards.

Now the "Auntie Ju's" started to turn back. They were too slow, too vulnerable to go any further. Below, searchlights began to sweep the sky. Flares hissed upwards. Here and there, forward ground troops ignited smoke pots as arranged. These were also signals for the attack force. Great red arrows of fire appeared suddenly in the snow. They all pointed westwards to the targets.

Inexperienced as they were, the eager young pilots, flying their first combat missions, were glad of any assistance to guide them to their objectives. They flew on. Now the "old hares," the veterans such as Colonel Buehlingen and Lieutenant Colonel Baer, waggled their wings. That was the signal for the young pilots to follow them down to the attack.

The four great waves dropped dangerously low. Still they kept strict radio silence as ordered. They skimmed across the barren, snow-sheeted landscape. Wherever possible they did what is called today "contour flying", skipping in and out of the deep, tight Ardennes valleys in order to escape detection by American radar. Soon they would attack and they wanted the surprise to be total. They flew on.

Later the surprised, crestfallen Allied fighter pilots would call it "the hangover attack". Most of them had been on a legendary binge that New Year's Eve. They were taken completely by surprise. Suddenly the icy-blue winter sky was full of German fighter-bombers. They seemed to be everywhere!

From Northern France to Holland, where the attackers succeeded in destroying Montgomery's personal Dakota, the intruders shot up airfield after airfield mercilessly.

Fighter ace, Wing Commander "Johnnie" Johnson, had spent a boozy New Year's Eve with his Canadians. Now feeling slightly fragile, he was watching as Canadian Squadron Leader Dave Harling, led a squadron of Spitfires down a slick, narrow runway through a field crowded with parked aircraft and totally undefended save by a handful of light ack-ack guns. Harling's task was to fly the morning weather reconnaissance. With his "Spits" behind him in a tight formation, he was just beginning a slow turn when it happened.

Without warning, a mixed bunch of some sixty Focke-Wulfs and Messerschmitts came zooming in at zero feet. Their cannon started pumping at once. Johnson who had just celebrated the wedding of Harling's pretty nursing sister only hours before, watched with horror, as three of the aircraft behind his friend were shredded into gleaming metal tragments within seconds. Frantically the pilots scrambled out of their wrecked aircraft and scurried for safety. Cannon shells erupted angrily around their hurrying feet.

Dave Harling opened up his throttle. He raced down the tarmac to take up the challenge. All alone he rose into the morning sky. He pressed his firing button. An enemy plane staggered as if it had just run into an invisible wall. Next moment it was falling out of the sky, trailing flame and smoke behind it.

Now the enemy pilots concentrated all their fire on the daring, lone Spitfire. Great chunks of metal flew off Harling's fuselage. White glycol began to stream from his ruptured Merlin engine. Within seconds it was all over. Harling 's battered Spitfire fell out of the sky, as the few guns defending the airfield grew silent – they had run out of ammunition. Now all Johnson and his fellow pilots could do was to watch in helpless rage as Spitfire after Spitfire burst into flames before their eyes.

Further up the field, stout Canadian ex-dairy-farmer, Frank Minton, was taking shelter in the Ops caravan when the phone began to shrill. Lying prone on the floor, Minton picked it up.

A frantic staff officer yelled, "Large gaggles of Huns near your field. *"Get your Spits off."*

The fear in the officer's voice was all too obvious to Minton. Despite his position, Minton's sense of humour didn't desert him. He yelled above the crackle of the German cannon, "You're too late! If I stick this phone outside you'll hear their bloody cannon." That was the end of that conversation.

The frightened staff officer was indeed too late. Ten minutes later the attackers finally disappeared.

Two-and-a-half hours later the *Luftwaffe*'s last great attack was over. The attackers had lost 232 pilots, nearly a quarter of the assault force. But they had wreaked a terrible vengeance on the "Anglo-American air gangsters and terrorists". At Brussels airport alone 123 aircraft, ranging from Flying Fortress bombers to Spitfire fighters, had been wiped out. At Eindhoven airport in Holland, used by Montgomery because it was close to his HQ, a Canadian Typhoon fighter-bomber wing was wiped out, plus nearly the whole of a Polish Spitfire wing. In all, twenty-seven Allied air bases were in ruins and over three hundred aircraft destroyed.

As the Free French ace, Pierre Clostermann, commented cynically, "This operation had been brilliantly worked out and superbly executed. Allied public opinion would have been dealt a staggering blow if it had been known. The American censorship and the press services, in a flat spin, tried to present the attack as a great Allied victory, by publishing peculiar figures. We pilots were still laughing about them three months later."

On that bright beautiful, but cold Monday morning of the New Year, Private O.B. Voss, who had been wounded badly on D-Day, was returning to the Continent from Folkestone. The draft landed at Ostend from an old pre-war channel steamer. The twenty-year-old veteran remembered many years later: "There were a couple of hundred of us, mostly green rookies, still wet behind the lugs, plus two Northumberland Fusiliers – both of them old sweats, who had refused to go into action and had been sentenced to seven years in the glasshouse. They'd had their sentence cancelled because Monty needed bodies for the infantry and they had decided to go back to the fighting. There were also a few Yanks, mostly black, who had now turned a delicate shade of green because they had been puking all the way across.

"Anyway we marched from the railway quay at Ostend across to the train, six abreast, blankets strapped around our big packs, singing our heads off. You could have thought we were old style Tommies in the Great War going back up the line.

"The train started. It was freezing cold. There were no windows. They were boarded up with just slits to see out of. We didn't get far, though. The train stopped sudden like. Everyone shouted the Belgie driver must have run out of wood for his engine. So there we were, in the middle of nowhere. Nothing but snow-covered fields to left and right. We stamped our feet on the floor to keep warm and of course when you're cold, you always want to take a leak. But our NCO wouldn't have it. "Piss out of the window!" he shouted. The Yanks didn't take a blind bit of notice. They got off the train and started wandering down the line to have a piss.

"I can remember to this day how the piss steamed as the Yanks took their leaks. Then all of a sudden it happened. A Jerry fighter came barrelling down the line, machine-guns blazing. The Belgie driver panicked. Christ, didn't he get that old engine going! We were off in a flash, throwing the lads inside all over the show. I thought the boiler would blow up, the way that Belgie was giving it throttle. And behind we left the Yank darkies, hands on their cocks, mouths wide open. God only knows what happened to them. That Belgie at the controls didn't stop again till we got to Louvain. For all I know they might be still standing there, waiting for the train to come back for them . . .

11

"It was only later that I got to thinking. I worked it out in my head. It was D-plus-177, one hundred and seventy-seven days, after I'd first gone ashore on D-Day, *and the Jerries were still bloody well attacking us!*"

They were indeed. After six months of very severe fighting, General Eisenhower's armies were still stalled on the German frontier. The Allied armies had lost three hundred thousand men killed, wounded or captured, plus a similar figure for non-battle casualties. Daily the "meat wagons" delivered their grim loads of dead soldiers to cemeteries all along the frontier from Margraten in Holland to Epinal in France. Already the rifle battalions, which suffered the most fatalities, had had a 100 per cent turnover in personnel due to casualties since D-Day. Now their ranks were filled with callow teenage greenhorns plus a sprinkling of "retreads", men who had been wounded, had recovered and had been sent back to the line.

And all that Eisenhower had to show for those tremendous casualties was a small enclave of territory around the old German imperial city of Aachen. Elsewhere German territory captured back in September had been retaken by the enemy in December during the course of the great German surprise offensive of 16 December.

By 1 January 1945, however, the Americans were beginning to go over to the offensive in the Ardennes. By now, though, the easy optimism of the summer had vanished; the GIs felt bitter and angry. Now they knew they were fighting for their very lives in miserable circumstances in the steep wooded terrain of the Ardennes in the worst winter in Europe for a quarter of a century.

It was a fight for survival, not only against the enemy but also against the elements. Medics kept their morphine syrettes from freezing up by tucking the little syringes under their armpits. Blood plasma was kept liquid by placing the flasks under the hoods of the medics' red cross jeeps. Their C-rations, they heated on the red-hot exhausts.

In the Ardennes the GIs learned how to heat food over a wine bottle filled with gasoline, using a twisted rag as a wick. Or they filled a can with a mix of earth and gas. Stirred to a porridge-like consistency this mix would burn and heat for a long time.

They learned not to eat snow to quench their thirst. That led to diarrhoea. Alcohol was dangerous, too. It led to a lethal cooling off of the body in those sub-zero temperatures. They discovered that metal sweated and then seized up, if the engines of tanks and trucks were not kept running at regular intervals during the freezing nights.

But most of all they learned how to *kill*, without remorse or pity. For they had finally shed one of the strictest taboos of western society – that killing is wrong. The average GI had absorbed his fear of aggression virtually with his mother's milk. At home and later at school he had been taught to be "a good boy". It had been one of the average GI's greatest handicaps when he first entered combat. For as military historian Brigadier General H.A.L. Marshal revealed after the war, "Only about a quarter of the fighting soldiers will fire their weapons against the enemy."

But the Ardennes changed all that – for those who survived . . .

By the beginning of January the equivalent of two-and-a-half British divisions were fighting alongside the "Yanks" in the Ardennes. In the lead was the British 6th Airborne Division. After suffering severe casualties in Normandy it had been sent back home to refit and to train for the crossing of the Rhine. But due to the fact that the British Army was scraping the manpower barrel and there were hardly any reserves, the Division had been hurriedly recalled to the Continent on 26 December 1944.

On 1 January, the Division's 13th Parachute Battalion was ordered to attack the Belgian village of Bure, which was the furthest point in the Battle of the Bulge to which the Germans had advanced. In heavy snow the lead company, B, formed up in woods overlooking the snowbound hamlet. To the left was A Company, with C Company in reserve.

As the commander of A Company, Major Jack Watson, recalled long afterwards, "We formed up on the start line and looked down on this silent and peaceful village. The Germans knew we were there. They were waiting for us and as soon as we started to break cover, I looked up and I could see, about a foot above my head, the branches of the trees being shattered by intense machine-gun and mortar fire. They obviously had the guns on fixed lines and they pinned us down even before we got off the start line. This was the first time I had led a company attack and within minutes I'd lost about one third of them. I could hear the men of the left-hand platoon shouting for our medics. We were held up for about 15 minutes because of the dead and wounded around us. But we had to get going.

"We were about 400 yards from Bure and so as soon as I could get my company together I gave the order to move. We had to get under the firing and get in the village as soon as possible. On the way down I lost more men, including my batman. One man took a bullet in his body which ignited the phosphorus bombs he was carrying. He was screaming at me to shoot him. He died later."

Somehow the little force got into the village, cleared a few houses and set up company HQ in one them. Here Major Watson learned A Company had also suffered severe losses. Its company commander had been killed. All the remaining officers had been killed or wounded, too, apart from Lieutenant Largeren, who was killed later in the day leading a grenade attack on a German-held cottage.

But Watson knew he would have to push on. In little groups the paras, in their red berets and camouflaged smocks, pushed down the village carpeted now with dead, British and German, "winkling" out the stubborn defenders. A grenade through the

14

window, a door smashed down; then a burst of sten gun fire through it. Inside, another burst to riddle the ceiling. Then that final mad dash up the stairs to the next floor.

But all the time Watson was taking casualties and now a new danger threatened. "Their Tiger tanks started to come in on us. It was the first time I'd seen the 60-ton Tigers and now here they were taking potshots, demolishing the houses. I moved from one side of the road to the other deliberately drawing fire. A tank fired at me and the next thing I knew the wall behind me was collapsing."

But a team carrying a Piat anti-tank rocket launcher came doubling up and destroyed the metal giant at fifty yards' range. So the battle for the insignificant Belgian hamlet went on and on until finally after forty-eight hours it was taken. Very tired, wet and unshaven, the paras withdrew. It had cost the 13th Parachute Battalion sixty-eight men killed and twice that number wounded, about one-third of its strength. They were buried in a field outside the hamlet a few days later: young men killed before they had really begun to live . . .

That same terrible week another airborne division, American this time, the 17th US Airborne, rushed to the battlefield, just like the 6th, from the UK, lost 4,000 men out of a total strength of 12,000, one-third of its effectives, in a matter of days.

It was the same everywhere. Whether attacking or defending, the Germans were fighting with that same old furious determination, skill, bravery and ruthlessness, as if this was that great year of victory, 1940, and not 1945, though, according to the Allied press, all was lost and Germany was about to cave in for good.

In that same week in which the two airborne divisions suffered their heavy casualties in the Ardennes, the 6th US Armored Division, which had served under Patton for six months, made its first tactical withdrawal since it had gone into action first on 1 August 1944. By sheer chance, just as their tanks started to

15

pull back under a grey, lowering sky, the Germans attacked. Panic broke out. In particular, the new replacements, who had just come up to fill the gaps in the Divion's ranks caused by the recent fighting, started to throw away their weapons. As more and more white-clad German infantry, supported by heavy tanks, came out of the forest, the replacements started to run to the rear. The withdrawal turned into a rout.

Colonel Hines, the son of a personal friend of Patton's and an officer who was soon to be grievously wounded and blinded himself, was in charge of the Division's Combat Command A. He ordered mines laid at once. Trip flares were also set. When the Germans stumbled over them, they would light up and reveal their presence – and also that of the panic-stricken survivors heading for his positions.

Alarming reports started to filter back to Hines' command. "The sole survivors" – in a rout there was always "the sole survivor" – reported whole outfits had been wiped out. There was no stopping the Krauts. They were advancing in overwhelming strength.

Of course these tales were wildly exaggerated. All the same this was the worst day in the history of the 6th Armored Division. Finally, however, some semblance of order was restored. Night fell on the battlefield and Colonel Hines, who would survive another three months before he was struck in the face by a German shell, found himself a little stone cottage where the men who had retreated were trying to thaw out and steady their shaky nerves.

One GI, his face covered with blood and dirt, his eyes two bitter, red holes, told Hines, "I used to wonder what I was doing in the Army. I didn't have anything personal against the Krauts, even if they were making me live in a freezing frigging foxhole. But I learned something this day. Now I want to kill every goddam Kraut in the world. You know why?"

The weary Colonel shook his head.

The infantryman rasped the answer harshly, *"To save my own ass!"*

It was a sentiment of which Colonel Hines heartily approved. All the same he knew, too, that the lone infantryman was in a minority. Morale was alarmingly low among the rest of the men. He didn't sleep too well that January night.

Neither did his chief General "Blood and Guts" Patton. That Thursday, 4 January, the normally optimistic and high-spirited commander of the US Third Army wrote sombrely in his personal diary, "We can still lose this war."

II

On that same Thursday, US surgeon Brendan Phibbs, serving with the 14th Armored Division which was engaged in heavy fighting in Alsace, recorded in his diary both his cynicism of the Top Brass and the suffering of the wounded.

"January 4, noon. Air at command post calm confident, where our division general and colonel nod helmeted heads above maps, discuss numbers of prisoners to be taken. Everything cool, professional, organized. 3 p.m. Ambulance loading post. The first casualties are coming back, soldiers groaning and babbling about their glimpse of the battle, their particular facet of a fly's view. 'We went past this town and we were near some buildings and a lot of artillery came down on us.'

'I hit the ditch next to the road and I felt this thing hit my ass and I couldn't walk.'

"A panicked white and blood-covered youngster keeps clutching my field jacket babbling, 'Am I gonna die, Doc? Am I gonna die?'

"Since his abdomen is torn with shell fragments, the odds are very good that he will. We get him out fast.

"3.30 p.m. Command post. General departed, likewise optimism. Air tense. Faces grey. Radio crackle confusion: patrol reports bridge in – wrong bridge. Key bridges are out; river deep, swift, infantry teetering across on planks, no way for tanks to follow. Heavy shelling. More casualties."

Dr Phibbs decided to motor up to the front and see where he could help. But he found his progress barred with heavy shelling coming in. So he attached himself to a battalion HQ, listening in to a distraught commander as he tried frantically to find out what was happening to his men.

"'Baker Company? Where are you? Phase One line? What? Not. Well then – where? Can you see me?'

"The answers aren't what they should be. The Colonel shakes his head and mutters."

The situation started to go to pieces disastrously. Instead of using code-names, the frustrated company and platoon commanders began to use personal names.

"Squawks and screeches predominate. Voices are rattled, occasionally incoherent. Someone is calling for weapons platoon. There's no answer but the caller keeps trying, rising to exasperation.

"Another squawk tells of artillery fire. 'I can't get my men to the fucking phase line because they're taking cover. Shelling. Sunray Six, what are you guys firing at?'

"'Bunch of fucking Germans over by those trees'".

"'Not our guys? I say again, not shooting our guys?'"

"The network explodes with a shout 'shit!'"

The distillusioned surgeon decided to attempt to get to the front again. But what he saw there only served to deepen his disillusionment and cynicism. As he wrote in his diary that day, "No attack . . . only the sudden, shattering loneliness of men dumped in the enemy's face . . . men until minutes before controlled by godlike figures, who fed, drilled, clothed them, moved them to the edge of danger and then left. Godlike figures suddenly shrunken to tiny voices, electronic dwarfs calling from the other side of the universe."

He concluded that, "In this particular battle, the gods are not only shrivelled. It seems the gods don't know what the hell they were talking about. Decisions are now up to lieutenants, sergeants, privates, organizing confusion, calling for artillery fire, siting machine guns, building defences . . . The battlefield has stepped in and is shaping the battalion's actions. Colonels and generals may as well bay at the moon."

However cynical and disillusioned he might be, Captain Phibbs kept his head and did his job of tending to the dying and wounded. On that same day T/4 Nelson of the green 70th Division did the same, when his fellow medics panicked and were about to abandon the wounded (even the chaplain ran away!). "Where will you go?" he cried as they prepared to follow the chaplain. "We're better off here" (he meant the Alsatian cottage which served as the aid post) "than out in the woods! Besides it's against regulations to leave the wounded unattended." He indicated the half a dozen or so men, moaning and tossing in their blood-stained dressings on the floor.

It was no use. Most of the medics fled, leaving Nelson and an unknown ambulance driver of the 45th Division to look after the wounded. Just then there was the hollow boom of metal striking metal. They ran to the shattered window. An American tank destroyer had just been hit by an enemy shell. Now it was burning fiercely, its crew running for cover under a hail of German bullets. Suddenly one crewman faltered. He flung up his hands in agony as if he were climbing the rungs of an invisible ladder. Next moment he slammed to the ground.

From a house nearby someone yelled frantically, *"Medic!"*

Nelson hesitated. He mumbled something about medics not being supposed to go in before the infantry. Then he asked the 45th man to go along with him. The 45th Division veteran rounded on him hotly. "Those fellows are doing the fighting in this war," he snarled at the greenhorn. "The least we can do is to pick them up when they're hurt!"

Nelson recovered his nerve. Another medic who had been wounded, rose from his stretcher to help. A doctor turned up out of nowhere. Together the three of them set about dealing with the dreadful casualties, which kept coming in all that

20

long snowy January day, with as Nelson remembered long afterwards, "the amputated leg with the combat boot still on it deposited next to the door, where it made a gruesome sight when the door was shut. We left the door open as much as possible."

Some simply couldn't take the strain. In the Alsatian village of Niederbronn, Major Ezra Silver, a 70th Division surgeon was working flat out to deal with the steady flow of wounded. They kept coming in all the time, torn, young, bleeding bodies, the floor at his feet slippery with blood, the bins overflowing with amputated limbs and human gore.

With the medics were the chaplains of all denominations trying to calm the fears of the wounded, soothing the dying, comforting the young soldiers as best they could. One of the chaplains was a Baptist minister, D.B. Webber, a man Silver didn't particularly like. He found him "a very stiff and unyielding person".

Now he stood at the surgeon's side as the latter completed the treatment of a young infantryman who had been badly wounded in the abdomen and leg. Silver pumped him full of morphine and now as the pain wore off, the boy opened his eyes and said to the surgeon, "Have you got a cigarette, Doc?"

To Silver's utter astonishment, the strict Baptist, who always lectured the men on the "vices" of drinking, gambling and smoking, took a pack of cigarettes from his pocket and placed it between the wounded boy's lips. He personally lit it for the soldier.

The latter took a few weak grateful puffs, while Silver watched the chaplain, fascinated by this sudden transformation. Suddenly, however, "every muscle in the boy's body tensed. His eyes rolled backwards and in a moment he had passed on – from a blood clot which had reached his lung".

Ashen-faced the Baptist padre went outside the aid station

and, leaning against the wall outside, broke down and wept bitterly like a heartbroken child.

Some – fighting men as well as chaplains like the one who had run away – simply could not bear the strain; the incessant noise, the constant threat of sudden death, the need to get up and advance into enemy fire. They broke down, fled into madness, convulsions or staring, catatonic silences from which they refused to return. "Combat fatigue!".

Medic Lester Atwell, serving with Patton's Third Army, was dealing with a fresh batch of wounded one late January afternoon, when he was startled to see a bareheaded soldier wandering around outside. He was wild-eyed and talking rapidly to himself. For some reason he was talking in French, then repeating in English the one single long drawn-out word. *"Noise. . . . The NOISE"*

After dealing with the wounded, Atwell took hold of the strange soldier and then told another medic to take him to battalion headquarters. "Tell them I said to let him rest up a few days around the kitchen," he ordered. "He'll be all right."

Then Atwell watched as the soldier – perhaps all of twenty-four – was led away, still whispering, *"The noise . . ."*

"Combat fatigue – a section eighter," he told himself and shook his head.

The two figures went down the road and disappeared into the gloom. Atwell never saw him again. Perhaps he had continued wandering, right out of the kitchen . . .

By now every division had its own combat fatigue treatment centre. Here the sick men were given a hot shower, a decent meal and some three days' drug-induced sleep in a warm bed. Then they were sent back to the firing lines. Some men went back and forth from the line to the centres like yo-yos. Montgomery, who now commanded more American troops than did any American general, allowed 'exhaustion centres', too, though he forbade the sending back of "bomb happy" soldiers (the British Army was much more down-to-earth on the subject than the American) to the UK. There, most of them, he knew, would make a remarkable recovery and "work their ticket" into civilian life, as did one soldier who later became a national trade union leader.

Some soldiers took even more drastic action than madness, feigned or otherwise, to get out of the line. They shot off their toes or fingers. Private First Class Hy Schorr of the 70th Division recalls a sergeant who was ordered out on a dangerous patrol. There and then, he whipped out his .45 and shot himself in the foot.

There were some who made pacts with each other. They would shoot off one another's big toes. When Patton cottoned on to this dodge, he ordered all suspicious cases to be examined by doctors. The soldiers countered by shooting their bullets through bread so that there would no tell-tale powder burns which would reveal this was a case of self-mutilation.

Others soldiers simply drifted away. They threw away their weapons and headed for the rear to the big cities. There they found themselves a "shack-up" job, usually a prostitute, amateur or professional; Paris, Liège, Brussels and the great continental cities to the rear were teeming with them. There they lived off the girl's earnings or their wits, working the black markets, using their knowledge and nationality to rob trucks of precious gasoline, even tyres, or perhaps the whole truck.

That January Eisenhower was shocked to find that there were allegedly 40,000 American deserters or men who had gone absent without leave in Paris alone. His shock was increased when he went to visit a hospital just behind the lines in Belgium and found all of its 1,000 patients were men suffering from self-inflicted wounds.

But still at the front hundreds of thousands of brave young men lived with the horror of combat, fighting bravely – and dying. They died in their scores, their hundreds, finally in their thousands. In the Ardennes and Alsace they were being killed at a rate of five to ten thousand men a week; the population of a small American township, let us say, vanished in a mere seven days. Whole regiments had vanished and in one case, the US 106th Infantry, virtually a whole division!

Back at the US military cemetery at Margraten on the Dutch–German frontier, apple-cheeked Captain Shamon, his white medical sergeants and his "darkies", as Shamon liked to call his black soldier gravediggers in the paternalistic fashion of the time, worked flat out. Each day the US First Army's "meatwagons" brought back the dead, splattering mud everywhere as the vehicles skidded and bounced their way to where the medical sergeants and the blacks, shovels in hand, waited for them.

Swiftly the sergeants went to work on the bodies, for no one wanted to leave the dead unburied overnight, however large their number. His "darkies" wouldn't have stood for that. Expertly the NCOs slit the two sides of the dead men's uniforms with their scalpels. All personal possessions were then taken from the dead and placed in little canvas bags to be sent home to the dead's kin. Dirty pictures, condoms and the like which might upset the dead man's loved ones were tossed to one side. Their dogtags came next. One was cut off to be dispatched to records in the rear. The other was placed in the dead man's mouth which was firmly pressed closed. This would help in any later re-identification.

That done, the bodies were handed over to the burial details who dug the graves. Earlier that January the ground had been frozen as hard as stone and sometimes it had taken up to four hours to hack away enough earth for a grave. Then even Captain Shamon and his second in command worked with the blacks to get the bodies interred before nightfall.

Surprisingly for the segregated US Army of the day, whites and blacks worked well together. This was unusual. There was absolutely no racial prejudice. Often whites and blacks prepared the same body together. Complications came only when they had to deal with the "X" bodies. These were bodies which had not yet been identified. The blacks hated working on them, for it was a gruesome business. For now, before they were buried, an attempt had to be made to identify them. First, fluid would be injected into the fingers in order to firm up the dead tissue. This would allow the sergeant to get a set of prints. Then the corpse's jaw would be forced open in order that a dental chart might be taken which could be compared with the dental records held in the States. Sometimes the corpse had neither hands nor head and the poor, battered body became that of an "unknown American soldier". There were many thus.

It was a ghastly business and one which might well turn the man doing the job into a corpse himself if he wasn't very careful. For the sergeants on the "stripping line", as it was called, were supposed to wear gloves. But they were too cumbersome for the job they had to do. Yet working without gloves on dead, putrid bodies, which might have lain on the ground for days before they were picked up, brought danger with it. The prescribed sterile techniques were almost impossible to maintain amid so much putrification. One day a sergeant might notice a blue streak running up his arm. There'd be hard knots under his armpit. Both were sure signs of the onset of blood poisoning and the NCO concerned would be hurrying off in the ambulance, with its siren screeching, heading for the nearest hospital himself.

That January Captain Shamon found he was running out of space and hadn't enough men to do the work. He was sent another company and then he motored over to the next US cemetery at Henri Chapelle near the Belgian-German border. He thought his opposite number, a Captain Pearson, might be able to take some of his dead.

He was mistaken. A weary Pearson told him his men were working day and night. They were still picking up thousands of American dead from the first week of the Battle of the

Bulge the previous December. He was running out of graves, too, and had already buried 15,000 US dead.

Sadly Shamon returned to Holland, knowing that he, too, would have to open up new fields. He did. Before he was finished he and his "darkies" had buried 21,000 men.

III

But the tide was beginning to turn slowly for Eisenhower's Americans in the Ardennes. For nearly a month the greatest land battle fought by the US Army in World War Two had been raging there. Now the US First Army, commanded temporarily by Field Marshal Montgomery, coming down from the north and General Patton's Third Army, driving up from the south in impossible conditions, were slowly cutting off the salient, "the Bulge", which had given the long hard battle its name.

On 16 January 1945, American Army photographer, Sergeant Douglas Wood, was alerted to move up to the front. He was told by his boss that two armies would be linking up and closing the Bulge just outside the little Belgian border town of Houffalize. The boss said this meant the Bulge would be "officially nipped out". That meant the Battle of the Bulge, which had cost the US Army 80,000 casualties and the British 2,500, would be over. This historic event had to be recorded for posterity – and the Press.

Wood fought his way up terrible, icy, snowbound roads and found himself crouching with some weary unshaven infantrymen of the First Army on the northern bank of the little River Ourthe which still divided the two US Armies. About an hour after he arrived a few cautious figures appeared, black against the snow, on the other side.

Some of the First Army men waved happily. The men on the other side took absolutely no notice of them. After a few minutes they disappeared again. Were they men of Patton's Third, the infantrymen asked themselves in bewilderment?

27

Some time later, six soldiers appeared. They waded the knee-deep river. They didnt seem particularly happy at the knowledge that this was a "historic moment". They were wet, tired and hungry. They said they belonged to Patton's 11th Armored Division.

Dutifully Wood took their picture. But he knew as he posed them doing the usual handshakes with the First Army men that he was wasting his time. A picture of "ordinary doughs" wouldn't be good enough for a press release back in the States. He decided to wait to see if something more exciting – dramatic – would turn up.

Then a senior officer appeared. Wood poised with his camera. This was better. The officer announced himself as Colonel Foy from a reconnaisance battalion. He waded across the river to where the tanks of Colonel O'Farrell's battalion of the 2nd Armored Division – "Hell on Wheels" – waited. Wood started clicking his shutter, yelling to O'Farrell, "Sir, there's a colonel here from the 11th Armored to see you!"

But if the photographer had expected something dramatic, worthy of this "historic" moment on the lines of "Dr Livingstone, I presume", he was sorely disappointed.

O'Farrell popped his head out of the turret of his Sherman, and Foy exclaimed, "Well, Jesus Christ, if it isn't O'Farrell! Haven't seen you since Fort Knox. Didn't recognize you in a tank."

That was that. The link-up had taken place. The Battle of the Bulge, the greatest land battle fought by the United States in Europe in World War Two, was over.

Now the battered German assault forces, which had marched into Belgium and Luxembourg so confidently one month before, started to pull back. They did so stubbornly, fighting for every bit of ground the Americans gained. Behind them they left their abandoned tanks and trucks, dumped for lack of fuel. They left a yellow trail, too, in the hard pressed dirty snow for all of them were now suffering from what the German "stubble-hopper" (infantryman) called the "thin shits".

If the American follow-up troops were hampered by the terrible weather – knee-deep drifts of snow, hills glazed with ice, a winter coming straight from Siberia – the Allied air forces weren't.

Near the German border town of Prum which the Americans had tried, and failed, to capture the previous autumn Captain Wilfred Crutchfield saw to his surprise that the road was jammed with German vehicles of all types. He brought his squadron of Typhoon fighter-bombers down out of the hard icy-blue sky and "found myself headed straight for a flak gun. I gave it a quick burst and knocked it out. Then I took a quick look at the situation and decided to bomb first on the curve of the road. I dropped my two wing bombs on the curve, tore big holes in the road and knocked out six trucks. This stopped the whole column deader than a duck."

Then Crutchfield and his fellow pilots went to work "beating up" the German column. "Hundreds of Jerries jumped from their vehicles and ran for cover. Others started to pull their vehicles off the road in an attempt to hide them in the trees. But the ground was snow-covered so it didn't do them any good. We followed the tracks and bombed and strafed them in their hide-outs. After my bombs were gone, we worked back and forth on the column and all hell began to break loose, as we'd knocked out the flak in the area and they were helpless. I've never seen as much confusion. The Jerries would run into the wood and then out again. They were like chickens with their heads cut off."

Captain Crutchfield was a man who obviously liked his work. But many had become like that since the start of the Battle of the Bulge. The Kraut was hated and the killing of Krauts was impersonal. The Germans were simply "chickens with their heads cut off".

29

Soon it would get worse. Soon these *Jabos**, as the Germans called the feared American fighter-bombers, would range far and wide across the border country, knowing that they had total air superiority. Not only would their pilots shoot up the "Kraut" soldiers, but their womenfolk and children too. Soon no one who dared to show himself in that proscribed, accursed country of Germany would be safe from the Allies' revenge.

In Alsace the battle still waged fiercely, with the enemy attacking and attacking yet again, even while their comrades in Belgium and Luxembourg were in full retreat. The hard-pressed Americans, many of them straight from the States and new to combat, had no alternative but to retreat. For a while they wanted to evacuate Strasbourg itself and de Gaulle declared that he personally, would ensure that if they did the Americans would not use French communications, especially the railway lines to and from the great Marseilles supply base. It took a hasty flight by Churchill from London to France to smooth away that problem. Strasbourg was not evacuated.

Still they retreated. The Top Brass decided to shorten the line. The American divisions in northern Alsace were ordered to withdraw over the Moder River. Somehow the locals seemed aware of what was going to happen. As the historian of the US 103rd Division wrote just after the war: "Just before the move the people of Alsace became strangely quiet. The shining joy was gone from the eyes of this liberated people . . . Tears welled in the eyes of young, and old Alsatians who had given up half their homes to the 'Cactus' (the divisional patch of the 103rd Division) asked hopefully, '*Vous nix parti?*'

Many of the 103rd soldiers, unwilling to break the news and under orders to say nothing, lied in reply, 'No, no,' they said, 'just shifting troops'."

The chronicler of the 103rd might have been romanticizing

* From the German *Jagdbomber* i.e. fighter-bomber.

30

things a little. After all, virtually all the able menfolk of Alsace were now fighting in the German *Wehrmacht*, including such infamous SS formations as the 2nd SS Panzer Division which had committed the atrocities at the French village of Oradour-sur-Glans the previous year. But the locals certainly knew the Americans were pulling out.

Those who had been with the Resistance told the GIs it would be certain death for them if the Germans returned. There were German spies everywhere. The GIs, in their turn, were angry. "Why pull back?" they asked. "Why leave these people to the mercy of the SS? Besides, won't we have to take back all this hard-won ground in the spring?"

It was no use. Orders were orders. Like thieves in the night, the Americans started to withdraw behind the Moder that afternoon, harassed by Germans dressed in American uniforms, so that no one trusted anyone. It was recorded in the 103rd lines that children, always a barometer of native feeling, began to hurl icy snowballs at the departing, shamefaced troops. The GIs didn't care much. "We deserve it", they told themselves.

It was no different in the villages which had been fought for so hard by the men of the US 70th Division. Jean Beck, then a youngster in the village of Niederbronn, now a professor at the University of Arizona, recalls: "Until January 20 it was pretty quiet at Niederbronn. The Americans retreated south-east in the direction of Pfaffenhoffen. All Sunday long there was not one soldier left in the town. However, during the night we heard shooting. On Monday about ten a.m. the Germans came from Philippsbourg. In front were a few cars pulled by horses, the Germans being out of gas. Then came a cannon pulled by horses. Everybody else was on foot. We could not understand why the Americans had retreated.

"For the sake of propriety and then for the salvation(sic) of what the Japanese call 'face'," wrote the historian of 222nd Regiment, it was a withdrawal. But in the minds and consciences of the men it was a retreat.

31

"It was cold that night, a bitter cold that ate into our bones. It snowed that night, a blinding blanket which wet us to the skin. We retreated that night, a retreat that hurt our minds. But worse of all was what our eyes told our souls. Our eyes saw people, newly liberated people, trudging down those snowbound roads with their houses on their backs and despair in their eyes. Hordes of civilians who had trusted us, moving once again to escape the imminence of a German advance."

Again the unknown chronicler might have been wearing rose-tinted glasses about the Alsatian people. But the GIs thought he was right. The Americans were running away, leaving these poor unfortunate people to face the music.

But, just as in the Ardennes a week before, things began to turn in the Americans' favour. The steam was beginning to go out of the German drive. In the East the Russians had started their great offensive towards the eastern frontier of the Reich with the former Poland. If nothing was done to stop them on the front, denuded of troops to fight the battles of the Ardennes and Alsace, the "Ivans", as the Germans called the Russians, might well drive to Berlin itself. Slowly the German High Command started to withdraw the panzer divisions in the West to meet the Russian threat. On the night of 24/25 January 1945, however, the Germans made one last attempt to force the line of the River Moder.

As the chronicler of the US 42nd Division's 222nd Regiment recorded, "We waited; all bammed and clattered, streaked and crashed around us" – he meant the German artillery barrage. "Shapeless blobs started to poke up out of their positions, moved round and started towards us. 'Spit on muzzles, sweetheart. Here come the devils!'"

But the "devils" didn't make it this time – altogether. Here and there their positions broke, but the mass of the Americans held, and continued to hold for the next forty-eight hours. It wasn't a victory really, but it meant that the Germans had about shot their bolt in Alsace.

*   *   *

32

He was a slight young soldier, very handsome in a boyish sort of way, with a freckled open face, keen challenging eyes and a helmet that seemed much too large for him. What was this teenage boy doing masquerading as an infantry officer, leading a group of men into action near the Alsatian village of Holzwihr?

In fact, the officer who looked all of sixteen, had been engaged in combat with the US Army's 3rd Division for nearly two years. He had fought in Sicily, Italy and now for four long months in France. He had been wounded twice already and had been awarded a dozen medals for bravery. He had been awarded a commission in the field for valour and he was said to have killed more men than anyone else in the US Army.

Only his eyes gave a clue to the nature of the man, as he slogged doggedly through the snow to the village, surrounded by his men, skinny bodies bent as if tensed for a sudden storm. They were sharp, quick, constantly on the move, looking for danger – and victims – like those of a predatory animal. As one of his closest and oldest friends would say long afterwards, "His appearance was deceptive. Beneath that shy exterior there was a keg of dynamite – with the fuse lit!"

Now the German resistance started to stiffen. There were German snipers everywhere, tied to trees, hidden behind barns. The grey sky, too, was full of the hideous howl of the German six-barrel multiple mortars, sending their huge shells to crash to the ground in a banshee-like shriek. Up front with his Company B, the young man with the baby-face, watched in horror as two other young men who had been commissioned with him the previous October, rushed for the cover of a steaming shell hole. Next moment it was hit by another mortar bomb. Their bodies were ripped to shreds. The two of them, he thought, hadn't lasted long as "officers and gentlemen".

Finally the shelling ceased and the weary young man and his company went to ground. They couldn't dig in – the ground was too hard. And they couldn't heat their rations. It was too dangerous to light a fire. So what was left of Company B, two officers, twenty-eight veterans and a handful of frightened replacements, huddled together for warmth and spooned out the cold, greasy hash from the ration cans.

Dawn again. The weary, frozen men stood to. They know the German habit of attacking at dawn. They fingered their weapons and eyed their front. Here and there nervous replacements urinated in the snow – a sure sign of jitters, the boyish veteran told himself. With their usual stomach-churning howl the enemy mortars opened up. The bombs exploded in bursts of angry red. Silver-gleaming lethal shell fragments hissed through the air. The other company officer, its commander, was hit. Now the boy was in charge. Two years before he had joined the same company as a baby-faced rookie. Now there was no one, save himself, left of that original company.

Midday came and went. A field artillery observer, a Lieutenant Weispfennig, came up and said he would give the infantry artillery support when the Germans attacked. At two o'clock that afternoon they did. The only armour the infantry possessed was a lone tank destroyer. Almost as soon as the German infantry came in view, supported by half a dozen tanks, the TD was knocked out, its crew fleeing for safety. The German infantry, two hundred of them, dressed in "spook suits" (white camouflaged overalls) and shrieking their heads off like men demented, pressed home their attack.

Hastily the young officer ordered his men to a prepared position half a mile back. He told Weispfennig to move back a little, too, and save the precious radio; he'd contact the artillery with his field telephone. Now the young man was all alone. Afterwards he would say of himself, speaking in the third person, "He had no idea of how he would ever get out of that spot, but for some reason he didn't give a damn."

So he waited there for the Germans to come, a baby-faced twenty-year-old boy, who was going to go down in the history of the US Army as its "greatest fighting soldier." His hour of destiny had come at last.

His name?

Audie Leon Murphy.

Now over the field telephone, headquarters could hear the boom and flat crack of the German 88mm cannon. One excited HQ sergeant cried, "Are you still alive, Lieutenant?"

Carried away by the crazy illogic of the battlefield, his uniform already smouldering from the burning tank destroyer, Murphy yelled back, "Momentarily, Sergeant . . . and what's *your* postwar plans?"

Now Murphy went to work on the German infantry. Twelve of them detached themselves from the main force and tried to outflank the lone defender standing on the deck of the smouldering TD. The young Texan, who had once said that as a kid if he didn't shoot accurately he didn't eat, spotted them. He swung the TD's machine-gun round and ripped a vicious burst at them at fifty yards' range. They went down like ninepins.

Now more Germans took up the challenge. As Weispfennig reported afterwards, "His (Murphy's) clothing was ripped and torn and riddled by flying shell fragments and bits of rock. Bullets ricocheted off the tank destroyer as the enemy concentrated the full fury of his fire on this one-man stronghold."

Another observer Sergeant Brawley stated, "The German infantry got within ten yards of the Lieutenant, who killed them in the draws, in the meadows, in the woods – wherever he saw them. Though wounded and covered with soot and dirt, he held the enemy at bay, killing at least thirty-five during the next hour."

Thus the one-sided battle lasted all that long grey afternoon until the Germans finally by-passed "the one man stronghold" and his field telephone link with the US artillery was severed. Then, finally, he dropped down from the smouldering TD, its turret and deck gouged a gleaming silver with the impact of the enemy shells, holes like the symptoms of some loathsome skin disease covering its metal.

His raincoat was full of holes. Yet not one bullet or shell fragment had penetrated his skin. It seemed he had come out of that tremendous, one-sided battle without a hit. Then he felt a dull throbbing in his leg. He looked down. His trouser leg was full of blood, but it didn't seem to matter.

Later he wrote, "As if under the influence of some drug, I slide off the tank destroyer and without once looking back, walk down the road through the trees. If the Germans want to shoot me, let them."

For that January day's events he would win the Congressional Medal of Honor, America's highest award. It would make Jimmy Cagney, the movie star, take him up and in due course he would go to Tinseltown, where he would make forty movies, mostly cowboy ones. "The only difference between them," he once quipped cynically, "is that they change the colour of the horses."

But Audie Murphy, hero and movie star, would never forget that day and all the other days in combat that had preceded it. The good comrades, with whom he had shared the tough, brutal, rough-and-ready life of the front, had all vanished, dead or broken men. Once he said, "You have a comradeship, a rapport that you'll never have again . . . You trust the man on your left and right with your life, while as a civilian you might not trust either of them with ten cents".

The fact that he was famous could never fill that void. The simple, if dangerous, but happy past had vanished. He never seemed able to recapture it. Like some latterday Gatsby, Audie Murphy was compelled to believe in "the green light, the orgiastic future that year by year recedes before us. It eluded us then, but no matter, tomorrow we will run faster, stretch out our arms farther – so we beat on, boats against the current, borne back ceaselessly into the past . . ."

*   *   *

In a strange way there were two young soldiers in Alsace that last week of January 1945 who were to become the two best known GIs to emerge from World War II. The one was a national hero, Audie Murphy. The other was a coward, the only man in the whole of the million-strong US Army to be shot for cowardice in that war, indeed the only American to be shot for that military crime since the Civil War.

His name was Eddie Slovik. Like Murphy he was a product of the Depression. He had gone hungry, too, but he had stolen to appease that hunger and had been sent to jail. This had given him a jail record. As he told his guards at his trial for repeated desertion "in the face of the enemy", they're gonna shoot me because once I stole a loaf of bread.

For months he had been in the stockade after he had been sentenced to death for desertion, waiting for Eisenhower's decision. In that same stockade were other men with similar death sentences. They were all convinced that their appeals against their conviction would be approved by Ike.

But this one time they were wrong. There had been too many desertions, too many men "bugging out" in the "face of the enemy". Ike ordered the sentence to be carried out.

Now on this last day of January 1945 in the Alsatian mountain village of Ste Marie-aux-Mines, Pfc Eddie Slovik, slight, sandy-haired and blue-eyed was going for his last walk. The 24-year old, watched by senior officers of his division, the 28th Infantry, and other high-ranking officers, was marched into the courtyard where he was to be shot, together with a Catholic priest muttering the Act of Contrition. He looked cold and his breath fogged the air, but he was composed, as if he had long accepted his fate.

His colonel, tough Texan, James Rudder, watched him without feeling. Later after the sentence was carried out he composed a message to be read out to all the soldiers of his regiment. In it he stated quite categorically: "Today I had the most regrettable experience I have had since the war began.

37

I saw a former soldier of the 109th Infantry, Private Eddie Slovik, shot to death by musketry by soldiers of this regiment. I pray that this man's death will be a lesson to each of us who have any doubts at any time about the price we must pay to win this war. The person that is not willing to fight and die, if need be, for his country *has no right to life"* (author's italics).

The execution of Private Slovik was all very formal. The firing squad lined up. Eddie was tied to the post. The witnesses, all enlisted men from the 28th, were to the left; the Top Brass to the right. As Sergeant McKendrick tied Eddie to the post with nylon parachute cord, the prisoner said, "I'm okay. They're not shooting me for deserting the United States Army. Thousands of guys have done that. They just shooting me to make an example of somebody and I'm it, because I'm an ex-con. I used to steal things when I was a kid and that's why they're shooting me. They're shooting me for bread and chewing gum when I was twelve years old."

At nine fifty-six precisely, General Cota, the commander of the 28th, gave the command *"Attention!"*

Captain Hummel, one of the witnesses who happened to be standing behind Cota, who was one of the heroes of D-Day, said later. "I don't think anybody who was there will ever forget one thing – the sharp crack of that volley echoing across the snow in those hills, followed by an almost perfect silence. Not a sound."

But Eddie was not yet dead, although eleven bullets had struck him.

The shooting was poor because the firing squad of his "comrades" had been nervous. All their slugs had missed Eddie's heart, marked by a white patch.

Dr Rougelot, the surgeon in charge, went forward to examine the target. He found Eddie was dying. He tried to drag out his examination so that the squad wouldn't have to fire again. But already the officer commanding the firing squad was ordering his men to reload.

That angered the surgeon and the chaplain. "Give him another volley if you like it so much!" the latter exploded.

Rougelot looked at the padre. "Take it easy, Padre," he said quietly. "None of us is enjoying this." Suddenly he slipped off his stethoscope. "The second volley won't be necessary, Major," he said to the man in charge of the squad. "Private Slovik is dead."

The chaplain anointed the corpse with oil, while the Graves Registration people stood by with the mattress cover to take away the body. During the wait Captain Hummel slipped across to Sergeant McKendrick. He indicated the "collapse board", which had been built to support Slovik in case he hadn't been able to stand upright. "It turned out we didn't need that bit of apparatus, Mac," he said thoughtfully.

"I came nearer to needing it than he did," the NCO answered. "I can't figure the guy out. If he was a coward, he certainly didn't show it today."

At ten-thirty that morning a priority message was sent to Eisenhower's HQ. It read:

TO: COMMANDING GENERAL ETOUSA
FROM: HQ 28TH INF DIV.
PURSUANT TO GCMO 27 HEADQUARTERS
ETOUSA 23 Jan 45, PRIVATE EDDIE D SLOVIK
36896415 FORMERLY COMPANY G, 109TH INF. WAS
SHOT TO DEATH BY A FIRING SQUAD AT 1005
HOURS 31 JAN 45 AT STE MARIE-AUX-MINES,
FRANCE.

January 1945 had ended the same way as it had begun – in blood and sorrow and sudden death.

FEBRUARY

"God, don't let this be a slaughter. Help them. End this!"

Medic Pfc Lester Atwell, February 1945

I

"If it moves, salute it," they quipped cynically, "if it don't, paint it white. For bullshit reigns supreme!"

This was Montgomery's British Army, which would now take up the challenge. It contained regiments which had a history going back two or three hundred years. Here men served in regiments in which their great-great-grandfathers had served at Waterloo. They had strange names – "the Old and Bold", the "Buffs" the "Death or Glory Boys" – and in their depots as recruits, the men of these regiments had sat on their bunks on a Wednesday afternoon on "a make-or-mend session", i.e. repairing their clothes or darning their socks, while a corporal lectured them on the regimental history and tradition. One Scottish regiment claimed to be so old that its nickname was "Pontius Pilate's Bodyguard".

Class and rank were supremely important. Each rank ate in its separate mess and officers were saluted at all times. There were even differences in rank and social status between the regiments themselves. North Country battalions, for instance, were much further down the social scale than, say, those of the Guards. The former even had grammar school boys as officers! In one battalion of Montgomery's Guards Armoured Division, the Scots Guards, there were a future British deputy prime-minister, a moderator of the Church of Scotland and an Archbishop of Canterbury!

But if the officers were of a different class to their men and took a paternalistic attitude to the "other ranks" – why, in the Guards a private soldier had to ask, "permission to speak, sir?"

before he dare address an officer – they looked after their men well. It was an officer's duty to see his men fed before he ate. It was also his duty to inspect his men's feet daily in combat to ensure that they were in order and there were no signs of trench foot or other foot diseases that come from long immersion in water. Unlike the more democratic US Army, where officers were less concerned about the welfare of the soldiers under them, trenchfoot never became a serious problem that winter as it did with the Americans.

The soldiers on the whole were a rough-and-ready lot, happy with what simple pleasures that came their way. An "issue" of one bottle of NAAFI beer or a looted egg, fried on the blade of a shovel would make their day. They spoke their own "lingo", dating back to the days when the British regular, "the old sweat" was accustomed to "getting his knees brown" in some far-flung corner of the Empire. For them "dollai" meant mad, "dhoby" to wash, a man was a "wallah" and a woman a "bint", and "char" was that indispensable beverage without which the average "squaddie" couldn't or wouldn't fight – *tea!*

During the six months' course of the campaign, they had incorporated some new phrases into their vocabulary. "Armoured pig" was spam; to get drunk was to be "zig-zag" and "to jig-jig" was to copulate. Anything stolen or looted was "liberated"; after all Montgmery's army wasn't called the "British Army of Liberation" for nothing! When they went to perform their natural functions in the wet and snowy fields, they "took a spade for a walk", because they used their entrenching tools to bury the faeces. Indeed the long-suffering British soldier was constantly digging. He dug holes to defecate in, to fight in, to sleep in – and sometimes to die in.

Wherever the infantry stayed for any length of time, they excavated regular pits for latrines, making a seat over the pit by means of a long pole suspended on two empty ration boxes. In deference to any civilians that might be in the area and who might be offended by the sight of so many naked rumps, they surrounded the "thunderbox" with hessian sacking. Fifty years on, one can still trace their progress in rural areas by those holes, together with the gun-pits and bits of shrapnel, which once formed the front line, marking the scene of some long-forgotten, hard-fought action.

They cooked over Tommy cookers, deadly little stoves which used petrol as a fuel. They had a nasty habit of exploding if they weren't kept clean. They also used large cans, filled with a mixture of soil and petrol, stirred to a porridge-like consistency. They were supposed to give a long-lasting, more powerful flame and they didn't explode on the soldier.

American rations had been worked out by some nameless genius in Washington and were calculated to give the GI 3,500 calories a day. But the average soldier was less than enamoured of them. That freezing February, a fruit bar for breakfast, washed down by a drink made from lemonade powder, followed by a Hershey bar, or worse "Hitler's secret weapon", the D bar, was hardly the kind of diet that prepared a soldier to give his all.

The British ate "Compo" (composite) rations: tins of "M and V" (meat and vegetable) stew; "Soya links", triangular skinless sausages made of soya beans which were fried in the grease they came in; lengths of canned fat bacon wrapped in greaseproof paper, which could be unwrapped like a sheet; and naturally "bully".

Corned beef was the "compo" rations' main component, together with "compo" tea, a crude ready-mix of tea, dried milk and sugar. The beef could be eaten cold on "dog biscuits", the ration biscuit (for bread was rarely available), fried as fritters, made into a hash, cooked as a stew, or even formed into crude meatballs by mixing the beef with crushed "dog biscuits". Yes, corned beef was highly prized. Even any available girls there might be in the villages behind the line were categorized by the number of tins of corned beef it took to win their favours.

"Char" served to wash this simple solid food down. It

was particularly prized when it was transformed into "sarn't-major's char". With the help of a can of evaporated milk, a bucket of ordinary "char" took on a deep-brown, rich, creamy look, in which a spoon would stand upright. But as the name suggests, this wonderful concoction was usually reserved for senior NCOs. GS (General Service) run was issued at half a mug a time per soldier when in the line. It brought tears to the young soldier's eyes and, in due course, probably took the lining off his stomach too. But it warmed and cheered and made life a little more bearable for a while; and then as the task of breaking open the "compo" ration case began, some slightly drunken wag would invariably crack the same weary old joke, "Which tin's got cunt in it Sarge?".

Now, while the Americans recovered from the ordeal of the Ardennes and Alsace, it was the turn of Montgomery's British and Canadians. Now they would be required to pay the butcher's bill. They would launch the first real, full-scale attack across Germany's frontier into Hitler's vaunted "Thousand Year Reich". There would be over 200,000 of them, grouped together in one corps – XXX Corps – commanded by General Horrocks, a corps which was as big as the whole of the pre-war British Army.

There would be five infantry divisions in the assault. They would attack across the border, through the *Reichswald*, the huge German state forest between Holland and the Reich. The five divisions had been in action since the start of the campaign. There was the 51st Highland, known throughout the Army as the "Highway Decorators" because they painted their "HD" divisional insignia on anything and everything. With them would be the 53rd Welsh, just returned from the fighting in the Ardennes, the 15th Scottish and the two Canadian infantry divisions, the 2nd and 3rd, which, made up of volunteers, had suffered the heaviest casualties of all Montgomery's troops, nearly 120 per cent of their original strength. In support would be the ill-fated 43rd (Wessex) Division, commanded by a general the troops called "Butcher" Thomas behind his back. In its rifle companies there had also been a complete turn-round of personnel due to 100 per cent casualties. The Guards Armoured Division would provide the tanks. Its officers kept "game books" recording their "bags" of dead Germans. Indeed one of its members, who would soon win the Military Cross, the future Archbishop of Canterbury Runcie, was asked many years later, whether he had actually ever saved any of his fellow human beings. He replied, "No, I've only *killed* them."

The Guards' divisional insignia was an eye set in a shield. This eye, according to the guardsmen, was supposed to wink when it saw a virgin. "So far," the big guardsmen were wont to quip, "it ain't winked once on the continent!" Where they were soon going, there would be no women for the eye to wink at or otherwise.

Now this massive army of men and machines waited in the dripping cold persistent rain on the Dutch-German border, facing the dark, sombre and sinister regimented lines of fire that made up the *Reichswald*. First they would have to fight their way through it, then the fortifications of the Siegfried Line, which elsewhere had stopped the Americans dead every time they had attempted to assault it for four long, costly months. Beyond the *Westwall*, as the Germans called it, lay their objectives, the towns of Goch, Cleves (from which that famous "Flanders Mare", as Henry VIII called his fourth bride, came) and Calcar. From there they'd advance to the Rhine to be ready for Montgomery's great set-piece crossing of Germany's last major natural barrier.

Some were lucky. They were billeted in villages, though houses and barns had their hazards, too. As Corporal Dudley Anderson remembered the time he spent before the attack in a rat-infested hay barn. "Live and let live was our attitude to them" (though on an earlier occasion a rat had fallen on his head so heavy that his "head swayed to and fro"). "As long as they didn't help themselves to your rations. We had enough killing on our hands without bothering about them."

Others were not so fortunate. They crouched in foxholes knee-deep in freezing water, not daring to get out even to attend to their natural functions. Instead they used empty ration tins. Men of the Canadian Nova Scotia Horse, for instance, lived "in caves and dugouts scooped out of the wooded hills". The field telephone, and food brought from the rear, were the Canadians' only contact with the outer world. For days on end they crouched miserably in their holes. "Some days," a Canadian subaltern recalled, "We lie in the mud . . . we eat twice a day, morning and night. Food is brought down a slippery path, mined along the fringes, under darkness and between scattered bursts of enemy fire, for they know our habits."

They were opposed by what General Rennie, commander of the 51st Division, soon to be killed in action himself, called bitterly "those bloody little para-boys". As Alastair Borthwick of the 51st's 5th Seaforths remembered them, "They were tough and obstinate and they fought like fiends." Once when attacked with flame-throwers, "they were still shouting, 'Come and get us, you English bastards . . .' We did not like the para-boys, but we respected them. They were good fighters."

Most of the teenagers who made up the First German Parachute Army defending the *Reichswald* were parachutists in name only. Only a handful of them had ever jumped from an aeroplane. Many of them, indeed, had never even been inside one! But they had quickly absorbed the ethic and young tradition of this special elite formation. One paratroop commander received every new recruit with: "From the moment a man volunteers for the airborne forces and joins my regiment, he enters a new order of humanity. He is ruled by one law only, that of our unit. He must give up personal weaknesses and ambitions and realize that our battle is for the existence of the whole German nation."

As an allied intelligence officer, ex-newspaperman Milton Shulman, summed up their quality that year, "Their faith in their Führer and their cause had not died. None of them had felt the sickening impact of defeat. They had not given way to despair and hopelessness that now gripped most Germans. Parachutists in name only they were. They had never been taught to jump from an aeroplane. The bulk of them had never received more than three months' (infantry) training. But they possessed two other compensating virtues – youth and a faith."

Their officers had, in some cases, fought in half-a-dozen countries on two continents – in Holland, Crete, Russia, North Africa etc. They were a hard, battle-experienced bunch, who had little respect for their Canadian and British opponents. They rated them higher than the *Amis*, as they called the Americans contemptuously. In a captured First Parachute Army assessment of the fighting value of Allied troops, it is stated that "the great victories in northern France have had a very positive effect on the morale of British and Canadian troops. However, it must not be overlooked that English army units can only achieve results when they are supported by large scale aerial support. If they lack this, then there is a great lack of offensive spirit in their soldiers.

"In summation, it must be stated that Anglo-American leadership in battle is based on superiority in *matériel*. An attack without strong artillery, aerial and armoured support is unthinkable . . . However, the English receive a very good training and even with the losses they have suffered so far, the reinforcements reaching the front from England are still well trained.

"Of course, one cannot compare the fighting spirit of the English or American soldier with that of the German. The German infantryman is far superior to them . . . The best example of this was at Arnhem where the Ist English Airborne Division was decisively defeated by our own ground troops because the English lacked their usual air and artillery superiority."

So now the "bloody little para-boys" waited for the English, or "Tommies" as they called them, to come in full force, as they knew they would. They knew, too, that in the thick woods their tank and aerial superiority would be of little use to them. In their prepared positions in log-covered weapon pits or in the thick-walled bunkers of the Siegfried Line they smoked their "lung torpedoes" (cigarettes) and drank their "nigger sweat" (black coffee), ate their "old man" (tinned meat reputed to be made out of the corpses of old men from Berlin's workhouses) and watched their front, the way the English must come. It wouldn't be long now, they realized that. At night they could hear the steady hum of traffic from the direction of Holland. Trucks bringing up ever more supplies and men. During the day they lay undercover, listening intently, as the little, light English reconnaissance planes droned round and round, trying to locate their positions. Oh, no, they told themselves, as they crouched in their hiding places, it wouldn't be long now.

From the Corps Commander, Horrocks, down to the humblest private, the men of the assault force were not sanguine about the bloody task that lay ahead. Horrocks, lean, ascetic-looking and very popular with his soldiers, who had led a very hard life as an infantry soldier (including years in German and months in Soviet captivity), knew the coming battle had been months in the planning. 446 freight trains had lifted a quarter of a million tons of stores to the battlefront. 100 miles of new roads had been built for the offensive and 400 other miles of road re-conditioned. Half a million, men including the 200,000 fighting troops, would take part in the attack, together with 35,000 vehicles. It was a tremendous effort, with Britain, back home scraping the barrel for equipment and manpower (Churchill had just called up 45-year-olds for the infantry).

All the same Horrocks, or "Jorrocks", as he was known to Montgomery, knew that with all the supplies in the world, for the biggest operation ever fought by the British Army he needed two things – "complete surprise and good weather".

He wrote after the war: "If the Germans got wind of our attack, they would move up their reserves before the battle started. But the weather exerted the biggest influence of all because the ground was frozen hard and if only the frost would hold on till February 9th, our tanks and motor transport would be able to go everywhere across country without difficulty."

The stage was set, the actors were in place, the drama could commence.

II

One minute to five on the morning of 8 February 1945.

All was silent, tense, dark. No sound save the wind and the drip-drip of the fine rain in the firs. Men crouched at their start lines. Some urinated. Others attempted a crafty "spit-and-a-draw". The old sweats had changed into clean underwear and avoided a meal. That way you stood a better chance of surviving if you were hit. Rookies had placed steel shaving mirrors in their breast pockets to protect their hearts. Others placed a Bible in their pocket. They had all heard of the man who had been saved by the Bible which had stopped the bullet penetrating his chest (he always seemed to be a bloke in another unit). And some prayed, but not many.

Lt Alastair Borthwick of the 5th Seaforths had already been "up for ages". For more than two hours he and his fellow Seaforths had been creeping around in the dark "checking weapons, sweating, shivering, stumbling into puddles and trying not to think too much about what the day might bring. From long experience (the 5th Seaforths had been fighting since El Alamein in 1942) most of us had learned that it did not pay to worry before a battle, that things turned out much the same whether one had the wind up for five minutes or five days."

Suddenly, startlingly, the greatest barrage of World War Two opened up. Horrocks was half-way up a tree at the time, his observation post. He was shocked. Later he wrote, "The noise was appalling and the sight awe-inspiring."

Borthwick wrote: "We had been told that we had fifteen

hundred guns to support us, now we began to see what fifteen hundred guns meant. A carpet of high explosive had been unrolled in front of 153 Brigade. The whole countryside was flattened."

The historian of the 4/7th Dragoon Guards was much more dramatic in his description of that barrage. He wrote: "It was a fantastic sight, never to be forgotten. One moment silence and the next moment a terrific, ear-splitting din, with every pitch of noise imaginable. Little bangs, big bangs, sharp cracks, the rattle of machine guns and the ripple of Bofors, intermingled with the periodic swish of a rocket battery. The night was lit by flashes of every colour and the tracer of the Bofors guns weaving fairy patterns in the sky as it streamed off towards the target."

Dazed by the tremendous bombardment the first prisoners told their interrogators that it had created "an impression of overwhelming force opposed to them which, in their isolated state, with no communications, it was useless to resist".

A German soldier's letter, captured later, stated: "When Tommy began his attack he started with such a terrific artillery barrage that we took leave of our senses. I shall not forget my experiences in the *Reichswald* for a long time."

"I was nearly blasted from my blankets by the deafening barrage of noise," Captain Foley wrote afterwards. "The ground shook with the fury of the cannonade and the walls of the sixty-pound tent whipped in and out like sparrow's wings."

All those who were there that cold, wet morning in February were very impressed by the tremendous bombardment put up by 1,500 guns, all except the *Sunday Times* war correspondent, Captain R.V. Thompson. "The most terrific barrage I have ever seen opened the Reichswald assault and went on for about forty-eight hours. It was the most staggering, awe-inspiring display of fireworks the mind can carry." Then came the sting in the tail, as Thompson continued, "*It killed about a dozen Germans!*"

*   *   *

In fact, the main enemy that day was not the Germans, but the mud. The Sherman tanks and other armoured vehicles which were to convey the great steel armada forward could not master the thick, deep mud. Only the Churchill tanks with their broader tracks could do that.

Still the infantry, dogged by the many minefields, kept on moving, bodies bent and tense like men walking against a tremendous wind. In front the curtain of man-made fire, a terrible creeping inferno which blew apart and incinerated everything in its path, swept forward lethally at one hundred yards every four minutes. To mark the end of each four-minute period, when the guns would increase their range by another 100 yards, all the cannon fired a round of yellow smoke to indicate the change. It was a tremendous technical achievement, co-ordinating the work of 1,500 guns linked by radio. At a time when "friendly fire" often killed more Allied troops than enemy, it exemplified the fact that, by this stage of the war, British artillery was the best in the world!

Now five divisions advanced abreast on a front of six miles behind that tremendous weight of steel, choked and nauseated by the overpowering stench of burnt explosive, but reassured that the stunned Germans, not even the "bloody little para-boys", had not yet reacted. Surely nothing could survive that tremendous maelstrom of flying steel and sudden death.

Captain Foley in his Churchill thought the same as his big tank crawled through the forest. In the turret Foley saw a captain of the Black Watch quietly watching the action, puffing thoughtfully at his pipe. "With his little cane and red hackle at the side of his cap," Foley recalled after the war, "he might well have been taking a Sunday stroll down Aldershot High Street except that vicious little spurts of dust were cracking about his heels."

"Look here!" Foley yelled down from his turret, "aren't you being shot at?"

"Oh never mind that," the Black Watch officer replied calmly, "it's only got nuisance value."

The Churchills ground on through the sticky mud, sending up a flying wake of wet earth behind them. Suddenly Foley heard a noise "like a small boy dragging a stick along some iron railings." A line of angry blue sparks dotted the side of his Churchill. Hurriedly he dropped inside the turret. "They've woken up!" he cried. Swiftly he looked through his periscope. He saw that the Black Watch were rapidly "melting into the landscape".

The real battle for the *Reichswald* had commenced . . .

III

On the frontier between Germany and Belgium, ravaged by the Battle of the Bulge the previous month, Patton prepared to go over to the attack with his Third Army. The weather was terrible. Heavy new snow fell, together with a tremendous, freezing wind. Desperately Patton's engineers fought to keep the road system from collapsing as convoy after convoy of the "Red Ball Express", driven by cheerful black drivers, brought up fresh supplies and equipment.

In the village of Lanzerath right on the border, Staff Sergeant Giles and his engineer company worked all out to build a bridge over the frontier River Our for the infantry to cross. "It was a bitch," he noted in his diary. "The river is 189 feet wide here and the chasm is 100 feet deep. The weather is lousy – snowing and blowing. And we had plenty of artillery fire. That's my idea of a real T.S. (tough shit). It's round the clock, boys and don't spare the horses."

Medic Lester Atwell, not far away in the German village of Kobscheid, noted that same day: "The captain paced up and down in silence, impatiently awaiting the word to move up further. Attacking the Siegfried Line, I thought, and prayed suddenly, 'God, don't let this be a slaughter. Help them. End this.'"

Atwell knew already that trouble had broken out in the ranks of the young men waiting to attack the *Westwall*. Riflemen were falling sick by the hundred, then by the thousand. Severe respiratory infection was decimating whole companies. Already the medical brass was setting up special hospitals just behind the lines to deal solely with chest infections. By the time the offensive got under way they would have dealt with the equivalent of a whole infantry division – 14,000 sick riflemen. And still it continued to snow, as if it would never stop.

The tension mounted.

General George S. Patton, the commander of the waiting troops, was unconcerned by the weather, the health of his troops or the fact that he would soon attack the Siegfried Line, which had repulsed every other American attack over the last five bloody months. Emboldened by his recent successes in the Battle of the Bulge, which had provided plenty of headlines in the States and had brought him back into the limelight again, he craved for further success. He knew, too, that the "little fart", as he called Montgomery, was making the running further north and would continue to do so, if he, Patton, didn't get his Third Army involved in a major campaign in the Eifel. For his sights were set on the Rhine, Germany's last natural bastion. Be first to cross the Rhine and he knew he would be certain of a place in military history. And there was nothing that Patton craved more than glory and lasting fame.

He was a strange mixture, "Ole Blood an' Guts" Patton ("Yeah," his troops quipped, "*our* blood, *his* guts"). Romantic and profane, brutal and easy-given to tears, supremely confident, yet subject to fits of near-hysterical uncertainty.

His standard speech to new troops went: "We'll win this war, but we'll win it only by fighting and showing the Krauts that we've got more guts than they have. We're not going to shoot the sons-of-bitches, we're gonna rip out their living goddam guts and use them to grease the treads of our tanks! We're gonna murder those lousy Nazi cocksuckers by the bushel-fucking-basket . . . Rip them up the belly! Shoot them in the guts! . . . We're gonna go through them like crap through a goose – like shit through a tin horn!"

Yet the same man wrote poetry and believed in reincarnation,

57

that he had been on earth before at all key stages in the development of human history; a dreamer, too, who believed it was his destiny to be *someone*.

Sacked by Eisenhower in Sicily in 1943 for having slapped a private soldier who he believed was a coward, he wrote on New Year's Eve of that year, "My destiny is sure and I am a fool and a coward even to have doubted it. I don't any more. Some people are needed to do things and they have to be tempered by adversity as well as thrilled by success. I have had both. Now for some more success . . . Destiny will keep me floating down the stream of fate."

Now, almost unrestrained by his immediate superior, Army Group Commander General Bradley, or the Supreme Commander, General Eisenhower, Patton was determined, come what may, to realise that destiny at last.

The first flares sailed effortlessly into the grey dawn air. For a moment they hung there, colouring the upturned faces of the waiting infantry a ghastly unreal hue. Then, as they dropped like fallen angels, the barrage commenced.

In an instant the frozen River Our was lit a startling orange, as the barrage descended upon the German positions on the heights beyond. A fantastic pattern of a myriad stabs and flashes of flame formed and died an instant later. In an urgent lethal morse, tracer zipped back and forth. Rockets whooshed into the sky, trailing fiery sparks behind them, fired from "mattresses" – huge banks of rocket tubes mounted on trucks. Here and there a maverick shell exploded and tossed up a ball of sudden fire like a roman candle. Shorts fell into the water, breaking the ice and sending the water up in angry white spurts. Awed and gaping-mouthed like village yokels at some monstrous carnival, the waiting infantry watched and waited for what had to come.

It came. Whistles shrilled. Red-faced noncoms bellowed orders. Officers rose to their feet, waved their carbines and yelled the old command, "Let's go, men!" Like very weary old men, the infantry rose from their foxholes and began to plod through the snow towards the river. Now the killing could start yet again.

The 4th Infantry Division, which led Patton's drive for the key Eifel town of Prum, had been this way before. That had been back in September 1944 when everyone knew the Kraut was beaten. Now they were going in again, with hardly a man left of those who had landed at Utah Beach on D-Day. Since then the Division had lost virtually 100 per cent of its original personnel. But the replacements were fearful yet optimistic. The Krauts had been shattered in the Ardennes. This time surely they would crack.

At first everything went well. Bleialf and the area where the ill-fated US 106th Division had fought, bled and finally surrendered the previous December became American once more. From there the infantry plodded up the steep roads to the heights on which were located the bunkers of the Siegfried Line. But first the plan was to capture the hamlet of Brandscheid, which had been integrated into the Line.

The officer who was to lead the 4th's attack on Brandscheid, was a small, bespectacled, white-haired colonel – "Buck" Lanham. Not only was Lanham a professional soldier who had led his regiment since D-Day – apart from time out for wounds – but he was also something of an intellectual. He numbered among his friends "Ole Ernie Hemorrhoid – the poor man's Pyle,"* alias Ernest Hemingway. Indeed Hemingway had attached himself to Lanham's 22nd Infantry Regiment the first time it had come this way in September 1944. But by now both Hemingway and that regiment had disappeared. It had been decimated in the fighting in the Hurtgen Forest, losing 2,678 men out of 3,000 and Lanham had agonized at

---

* A pun on the name of the GI's favourite reporter Ernie Pyle, a man Hemingway detested.

the time, that "my magnificent command has virtually ceased to exist!"

This time, however, Lanham determined there would be no slaughter of his men at Brandscheid. Once his men had cleared the eleven pillboxes guarding the approach to the hamlet, his assault companies would attack well supported by armour. Let the tanks, who had let them down so often in the Hurtgen earn their pay for once.

On 5 February, Lanham attacked. Under heavy mortar and artillery fire, one of his three battalions spent the morning clearing the pillboxes. Then ten Sherman tanks and seven tank destroyers, armed with huge 90mm guns, rumbled up. Precisely at midday, they opened fire on all visible pillboxes guarding the road to Brandscheid itself.

From the woods heavy machine-guns and mortars joined in. Tracer whizzed back and forth, a dazzling white. Shells bounced off the thick hides of the tank destroyers like glowing ping-pong balls. Mortars howled obscenely. Great steaming brown holes appeared in the fields nearby like the work of gigantic moles.

Now it was the turn of Lanham's infantry. They burst out of the fir trees shouting and yelling like men demented. As they ran and stumbled through the snow, they fired from the hip, "marching fire", it was called, lobbing white phosphorus grenades in front of them. Speedily they closed on the now burning hamlet.

At first the second-rate "people's grenadiers" holding the ring of pillboxes around Brandscheid returned their fire. Then their fire started to slacken. More and more of the dirty, lice-ridden defenders began to emerge crying *"Kamerad"*, knowing that if they waited till the *Amis* stormed their bunker it would be too late. They would be shot where they stood. These days the Americans weren't inclined to take prisoners.

In three short hours it was all over. Lanham had taken a formidable Siegfried Line position at the cost of forty-three wounded. But it wasn't all over yet. The Germans would be back.

The German counter-attack came at four in the morning.

It was a miserable night. The rain came down in sheets. It was intermingled with sleet as the US infantry came slogging up the slushy road from Bleialf to Brandscheid cutting their faces like a myriad sharp knives. For one of the most dangerous of military exercises was taking place. The 22nd Regiment was being replaced by 358th Infantry of the US 90th Division.

Now the new boys assembled in the ruined hamlet, while the officers exchanged information on the position. Odd soldiers wandered off "to take a crap" . . . "find a cup of Java (coffee)" . . . "somewhere where I can get my frigging blisters treated . . ."

Startlingly, suddenly, it happened. Without even a preliminary bombardment, the Germans attacked from the south. Over 400 of them. They came running out of the night. Schmeisser machine-pistols barked. Stick grenades exploded. Abruptly all was confusion and sudden death.

Lanham's Company K was shattered immediately. The panicked survivors fled into the hamlet, yelling, "The Krauts are coming, the Krauts are behind us!"

And they were. As usual the Germans were lightning-quick, eager to take advantage of the new situation. They flooded right into the centre of the village, right behind the survivors of Company K. Here and there a rifleman of Lanham's 3rd Battalion to which the company belonged, tried to hold them. But the Germans' dash was too strong. Lanham's men began to pull out of Brandscheid.

Lanham, the veteran, was equal to the situation. He didn't panic. He rallied his Company L, the only one in the 22nd which had completed the handover. It went into the attack. Fierce hand-to-hand fighting broke out. Men pelted from door to door down the cobbled street. Grenades hissed through the air and dead snipers flopped from upper floors like sacks of wet cement.

In the end the Germans gave in. More than 150 of them surrendered as another grey dawn broke. But the cost to the Americans had been high. The men of the 90th Division had suffered only nine fatalities. But Lanham's 3rd Battalion had lost one fifth of its strength in two short hours. That grim grey dawn Lanham must have wondered whether his beloved regiment's luck had run out yet again.

A score of miles away to the south, three other of Patton's divisions, belonging to the corps commanded by portly General Eddy were also preparing to cross a border river into the Reich. From Luxembourg they would assault across the frontier-river, the Sauer, between the townships of Echternach and Bollendorf. Two of those divisions, the 80th and 5th Infantry were veterans. The 76th, on the other hand, which was green and contained some of the first black troops to go into action, had never been in action before.

The veterans of the 80th kicked off the attack. They attacked at one in the morning under light snow. Almost immediately the men of the initial wave ran into trouble. The light rubber dinghies, captured from the German *Luftwaffe*, hadn't a chance in the fast wild water of the River Sauer. A lot capsized at once. Others careened back to the western bank.

A few determined, men, however, pushed on till they reached the other bank. But the screams of the men drowning in the river had alerted the enemy. A single rifle shot rang out. It seemed to act as a signal. Suddenly the whole eastern bank erupted into hectic activity. Star shells burst above the Americans still trapped in the middle of the river. The slaughter had commenced.

It was no different in the 5th Division sector. The veterans of a dozen river crossings had run straight into German fire from the steep heights beyond the Sauer River. The enemy couldn't miss at almost point-blank range. The infantrymen in their frail rubber boats were sitting ducks. Numbly the trapped infantrymen accepted their inevitable fate like dumb animals.

Organization fell apart. Now it was every man for himself. A house on the Luxembourg side went up in flames. It turned night into day. It outlined the men struggling for their lives in the water against its scarlet backdrop.

A medic, Private Harold Garman, was one of those trapped. A moment before a burst of German machine-gun fire had struck his boat. Four of the men with him were wounded. The rest dived overboard, leaving the wounded to their fate. Not Garman. He slipped into the icy water and started to push the boat, with its moaning and groaning cargo of misery, back to the American side. With enemy bullets twitching and plucking the water all about him, he made it.

Later when Patton presented the young medic with America's highest honour, the Congressional Medal of Honor, he asked Garman, why he had done it. Garman (in Patton's words) "looked surprised and said, 'Well, *someone* had to do it, sir.'"

Now it was the turn of the 76th Infantry Division. Exactly ninety days before the division had been attacking a simulated foe in the peaceful hills of Wisconsin. Now they were going to attack the real thing.

All night long artillery pounded the German-held heights at Ferschweiler which dominated the assault area so that the Germans could see everything going on at Echternach, from whence the Americans would attack (and from whence in the 9th century an English monk, St Willibrod, had sallied forth to convert the heathen Germans on the other side of the river).

The staff already knew that the 5th Division's assault had failed. Only two boatloads of troops from that division had reached the other side, a total of sixteen badly frightened men. Still the staff knew they had to make the attempt, although this was the position most strongly held by the enemy.

The lead company pushed off. They prayed the noise of their own artillery might drown any sound they might make. Each man was wrapped in a cocoon of his own thoughts. The minutes passed in nerve-tingling, electric apprehension, as they plied their paddles against the fast-flowing current. Above them on the heights the Germans remained strangely quiet. Perhaps they were going to make it after all.

A sudden whoosh. A sharp crack. Above them a star shell exploded. It cast everything below in its harsh silver light. They had been spotted!

Almost immediately the massed German machine-guns opened up. Red tracer zipped towards the hapless men in the frail boats like flights of angry hornets. Desperately the Americans crouched low and paddled with all their might. But as mortar bombs started to fall into the river, many panicked. Men jumped overboard. Others swamped their boats. There were dying and wounded everywhere as boat after boat was struck.

Most of the men were carried away by the current, laden down by their equipment, till they drowned. One, Private Harry Goedde, was a strong swimmer. Somehow he fought his way to the opposite bank. There, he watched helplessly with another wet shivering survivor as the second wave was slaughtered by the enemy just as the first one had been. In the end just over 100 men of the two companies, some 250-strong, reached the far bank. In its first combat action the 76th Division had suffered over 50 per cent casualties of the men involved. Thus as dawn broke it seemed that Patton's first major venture, with four divisions, into Hitler's Reich was a failure.

Patton was angry. Not only had the river crossing failed, but he had just received word that as soon as "the little fart's" operation in the north got fully underway, his own operations would have to cease. Apparently there was not enough ammunition for two major drives into Germany. In addition, his Third Army would be required to transfer several of its infantry divisions to General Simpson's US Ninth Army, which would be fighting under "the little fart's" command.

Immediately Patton summoned his corps commanders to his HQ. He told them the situation and that Montgomery was going to have priority soon. But he revealed to them, too, that he was going to have his own way, even if it did mean disobeying Eisenhower. "Personally," he said slowly in that squeaky voice of his, "I think that it would be a foolish and ignoble way for the Americans to end the war by sitting on our butts. And, gentlemen, we are not going to do anything foolish or ignoble . . . Let the gentlemen up north learn what we are doing when they see it on their maps."

Now he ordered his corps commanders to pull out all the stops. He wanted the drive into the Reich to succeed, and quickly!

It was the old trick. The corps commanders put the pressure on their divisional generals. They, in their turn, did the same to their regimental commanders, who put pressure on their battalion commanders. So it went on until frightened private soldiers such as a Private Ulrich found themselves wandering around, weaponless and alone on the German side of the River Sauer, being fired on all the time. As he reported later, "It seemed to me that I was the only Yank in Germany and that the whole *Wehrmacht* was zeroing in on *me!*"

Gradually the number of Americans on the other side of the river grew and grew and a bridgehead was formed. But the river still remained a problem. Two days after the first attack, there was still not a single bridge across the Sauer in the 5th and 76th Divisions' sector. There was not even a telephone link. Two volunteers tried to swim a line across but were stopped by floating mines. Someone came up with the ingenious idea of firing a rope across by means of a bazooka rocket. It worked, but German artillery cut the rope.

Finally a telephone link-up was made and now the staff

heard just how perilous the situation was on the other side. Food and ammunition were needed urgently. Casualties – and there were many of them – had been lying in the snow and mud for thirty-six hours. Dog teams were rushed up, but they were still unable to cross the river. In the end the commander of the 76th Division ordered all available artillery spotter planes to ferry urgently needed supplies to the other bank. But they were not to land to bring out the wounded. The wounded would have to fend for themselves.

The 5th Division got lucky. Under fire, its engineers managed to throw a bridge across the Sauer. It was immediately shrouded with a thick smoke screen. Patton went up to have a look at once. Spick and span as always in his elegant uniform and lacquered helmet with its outsize stars plus the famous pistols, his presence was greeted with astonishment by his hard-pressed troops. They knew nothing of the new bridge across the Sauer. So how had "ole Blood an' Guts" got across?

Wild rumours started to circulate almost immediately. *Patton had swum the Sauer single-handed*! As the soldiers' newspaper *Stars and Stripes* recorded the incident: "A fighting front is the breeding place for wild stories. Here is one from this sector. Out of the misty night appeared General George S. Patton Jr. 'Call back the boats!' he screamed. 'They will make too high a silhouette. *We will swim*!' The boats turned in mid-stream. The GIs climbed on to the west bank. They hesitated. The General acted. He waded deep into the river and struck out with a powerful crawl. Halfway to the other side, he turned his head and waved. The inspired troops dove in and swam across."

Patton must have loved it.

Now the Our–Sauer River line had been forced. In front of Patton there was just the River Kyll. Thereafter came the big one – the Rhine, the most glittering prize of all. But the task of forcing that first river line had taken its toll. By the end of February, many of Patton's men were exhausted, worn down by the terrain, the weather and the enemy.

Veterans such as medic, Lester Atwell, and his comrades no longer cared about anything. Just behind the front, they attended – in a shell-shattered church – a break in the murderous routine of the line. They watched Abbott and Costello in *Lost in a Harem* and Rita Hayworth in *Cover Girl* four times over on the same day until the Catholic padre complained.

"At that time," Atwell noted, "no one seemed to care about anything. Sentences went unfinished, listening faces were loose and vacant, everyone yawned, sprawled, wrote letters in a desultory way, waiting for one tiresome, not quite sufficient, meal to follow another. The men hung around the sacristy, crawling over each other like puppies. It was all, 'Go wan, ya f . . . Aaah, ya f . . . Git yer feet off me, ya greasy bastard . . . Ah'm telling you, boy, if Ah ever gits home for a furlough, they're gonna have to burn the woods and sif' the ashes to find *me* again!'"

Others were apprehensive about what was soon to come. Staff Sergeant Giles, an engineer, found himself in a desolate stretch of the now quiet battlefield – "nothing but stumps of pine trees, limbs all blown off, upper halves splintered". He found it "weird and spooky and gave you the creeps". But what the immediate future held worried him more. "This is the part of the war I have dreaded the most. I even dreaded crossing the border and knowing I was in Germany. I have always thought the Krauts would fight like devils for every inch of German soil – and in a way they are. I dreaded this Siegfried Line. I still dread the Rhine. It stands to reason. They have their backs to the wall and that lunatic Hitler will fight till the last German is dead before he gives up."

III

In the Reichswald, the slogging match continued. All the time the British and Canadian divisions were attacking through pouring rain. The Germans, defending the battered waterlogged terrain, were in a dilemma for which there was no solution. They knew the Americans would soon achieve a breakthrough further south. But if the British advance under Montgomery was left unchecked, it would be just as serious a breakthrough. Montgomery would head straight for the industrial heart of Germany, the Ruhr, and then on to the Reich's head, Berlin. *They had to stop the British.*

They blew the Roer dams opposite Simpson's US Ninth Army, and sent eight divisions from that front further north to counter the threat posed by Montgomery.

They opened the banks of the Rhine, too. Immediately, the battlefield began to be swamped. That week R.V. Thompson reported to the *Sunday Times* that the battlefield had become "practically a naval action". He noted: "the tops of houses, the turrets of derelict tanks, smitten tree trunks and the branches of telegraph poles, and all the fearful garbage of war gave shape to all this desolation of water. Otherwise it might almost have been the sea."

The soldiers now quipped they were "the water rats" (a pun on "the desert rats" of the war in Africa). They went to battle by boat and at night formed their "laagers" on the small islands of mud above the water level.

Taking up food to these isolated outposts could take up to eighteen hours. Captain Quartermaster J. Moore of the East

Lancashires recalled after the war trying to get up warm food to one of his companies. "No roads could be seen, or even signs of any. It was just a lake . . . We could have got through because I had a pretty good idea where the submerged road was, but our luck was out and Bean, the driver, ran into one of the Jerry slit trenches. No one would stop to help – you couldn't blame them. So I got out and tried to make my way on foot. The water was up to my thighs and the Dukws kept giving me their wash, but I survived." He did, but the men of that particular company of Lancashires didn't get any hot food that day.

Bereft of their armoured protection, the long suffering PBI (poor bloody infantry) faced not only the mud and water, but mines. Of all the weapons employed during the Second World War, the mine was the one most feared by the ordinary footslogger; and no one was more efficient in employing them in a defensive position than the Germans. They came in all shapes and sizes, from what the Americans called a "bouncing Bessy", a small anti-personnel mine, to the big Teller mine, the size of a small dustbin lid, which could take the metal belly out of an unwary tank.

But the Germans did not employ mines alone. They were experts at booby-trapping them. Mines were linked to other mines by hidden wires. Even if the first mine was successfully disarmed it would explode the second one. They used matchbox fuses, a steel contraption held closed by a powerful metal spring. This was placed beneath the mine. When the latter was lifted, the matchbox fuse went off. The result – yet another death or terrible disfigurement.

Naturally most mines could be detected. But by now the Germans were using mines housed in wood, glass and bakelite, an early form of plastic, which couldn't be detected by the engineers with their detectors.

"The minefields leading up to the Rhine were the worst sods I ever saw," ex-Royal Engineer Alf Jones recalled nearly fifty years later, the horror still evident in his voice. "The buggers were everywhere. So many, that the infantry had to go for them themselves, crawling through muck on their bellies, prodding at it with their bayonets. Then when they found them, digging them up, sweating like pigs. But that wasn't the worst of it. Up to the Rhine those bleeding paras of theirs always sited a machine-gun to cover a minefield . . . So the poor sods of the PBI had to do all this crawling on their bellies with the bullets cutting the air just above their heads. No bloody picnic, I can tell you."

Now the British and Canadians were taking 1,500 casualties every single day. They were flooding the military hospitals right across Belgium right back to the UK itself. "Let no one misconceive the severity of the fighting during those final months," Colonel Stacey, the Canadian military historian, wrote after the war. "In this, the twilight of the Gods, the defenders of the Reich displayed the recklessness of fanaticism and the courage of despair. In the contests west of the Rhine, in particular, they fought with special ferocity, rendering the battles of the Reichswald and Hochwald grimly memorable in the annals of this war."

Canadian casualties, indeed, were horrendous. Right up to 1945 all Canadians serving overseas had been volunteers. Now the Government was trying to send pressed men overseas. But they weren't having it. Desertions at the ports of embarkation were widespread. So the embittered volunteers, growing fewer in number by the day, had to live, so to speak, off their own fat. Everyone, who could hold a rifle – cooks, clerks, drivers – were given a day or two's training and became instant infantrymen. But unlike the vets, who knew the lethal rules of battle all too well, they didn't last long.

General Simmonds, an officer well liked and admired by Montgomery, who thought little of the older Canadian generals, commanded the 2nd Canadian Corps on Horrocks' left flank. He was staff college trained, an expert in modern mobile

70

warfare. But here he was required to fight a battle that reminded older Canadians of the battles of the Great War, Vimy Ridge and Passchendaele. And just as they had shown their courage in that war, they did again in this. The fact that several Victoria Crosses were awarded to Canadian soldiers within a few days, is testimony to both the bravery of the "colonials", as the stuffier British liked to call the Canadians, and the savagery of the fighting.

Sergeant Aubrey Cousins, for instance, who with four other Canadians held off a German attack by paratroopers. Once the Germans had gone to ground, Cousins became a one-man army. He charged the house in which the Germans had taken cover, killing twenty of them and capturing many more. There the NCO consolidated his position, told his four exhausted men he was going back to report to the CO and was five minutes later shot dead by a German sniper.

Major Tiltson was another Canadian who won the Empire's highest honour. Leading his men of the Canadian Essex Scottish into the attack in the last week of February over an open field and through a series of barbed wire obstacles, he was shot badly in the head. For a while he was confused. Still he continued to lead his company. Suddenly a machine-gun nest loomed up out of the fog of war. He silenced it with a well-aimed hand-grenade. He and his Essex Scottish pressed on. Tiltson was hit again, this time in the hip. He collapsed on the ground. Still he didn't give in. He continued to direct his men as they cleared the German trenches, a mass of sweating, swearing men in field grey and khaki, swaying back and forth, giving no quarter and expecting none.

The German paras rallied and counter-attacked. Tiltson organized his survivors. They were down to a quarter of their original strength by now. Still the Canadians slogged it out. Tiltson was hit yet again. He refused to be evacuated. He lay in a shell-hole, half-filled with water, and kept on fighting. Finally the Germans were driven off. Then and only then, did the brave Major allow himself to be evacuated. He, too, won the VC but it cost him a great deal. Both his legs had to be amputated.

In the end the price paid by the 1st Canadian Army was severe. But the majority of the casualties were British – 770 officers and 9,660 men; the Canadians lost 379 officers and 4,935 men, most of them being lost in that last week of February 1945.

Mostly and mercifully, death came easily at the front. The crack of a sniper's rifle, the high-pitched hysterical hiss of a German machine-gun, the shriek of an 88mm like a huge piece of canvas being ripped apart violently and the victim would be dead. The wounded were another matter. Face ashen, eyes wide and wild with shock, he'd lie there in the mud or snow, clutching a bleeding, shattered limb while an angry hoarse voice would bellow "over here . . . stretcher-bearer . . . *over here!*"

Then he'd be in the hands of the medics, ripping at the tattered, blackened, bloody khaki with their knives, pressing home syringes that looked like toothpaste tubes with pins at the end, applying clumsy, thick, yellow pads, with their khaki-brown bandages.

Soon boxlike ambulances would appear, in their window a little sign proclaiming, "Priority One – carrying casualties." Off they'd go, with the wounded man strapped inside, bouncing and bumping across the churned-up fields. A forward dressing station. Harassed doctors, with perhaps a blood-stained apron around their loins, working in the white hissing glare of a petroleum lantern, cutting, slicing, excising, patching, ensuring that the wounded man would survive the next stage of his long journey.

Wound tags would be pinned on them, the morphia dosages and other medical details pencilled on foreheads creased with pain and then they'd be off again, carried ever westwards in a strange white haze, their nostrils full of the smell of disinfectant and faeces.

More doctors, senior ones this time. Feeling their pulses, ripping off clotted dressings mercilessly, sniffing at the gaping wounds for the sweet, cloying stench of gangrene. Here a few of the wounded would be given the coveted "red disc". This meant they were seriously wounded and would be sent to the UK for further treatment. This was "the blighty wound", that many of them had longed for. Soon the wounded man's relatives would be receiving a buff War Office telegram marked *Priority*, and would undoubtedly worry themselves sick.

The rest would remain behind in one of the big field hospitals in Louvain or Brussels, spending the first few days in a drugged sleep. Those with broken limbs were often roped in strange postures; all of them were swathed in great bloodstained dressings stinking of foetid, broken flesh. Moaning and groaning in their drugged sleep, they would relive, screaming and shouting out orders and fear, until they slipped into the blessed oblivion of deep sleep.

But not all the patients in these general hospitals were wounded from the front. There were the "leadswingers", too, all busy trying to "work their ticket". There were men who had rubbed diesel oil into their chests to cause an incurable eczema. Others industriously swallowed soap before every medical inspection. It gave them a high temperature and set their heart beating at a tremendous rate. Some had a hidden rubber ball which, when none of the hospital staff were looking, they kept for hours underneath their armpits to induce a temporary paralysis, good enough, they hoped, to fool the medics and get them sent back to "blighty".

But soon both the genuinely wounded and the leadswingers would be going to the front. Montgomery was running out of "bodies" and everyone who could hold a weapon was needed. Already he had "cannibalised" two infantry divisions to provide riflemen to fill the terrible gaps caused in the ranks of his fighting troops. In addition, he was "stealing" two divisions, one Canadian and one British, from the Italian front to help out. Soon he'd have all rear echelon units, including hospitals, stripped of men, even if they were not quite fit; for Montgomery was closing to the Rhine at last and soon there would be another great battle to be fought there.

Some went back reluctantly, especially the "leadswingers". But most were happy to be back with their old comrades. As one officer, wounded in the earlier stages of the campaign, expressed it as he returned to his old company: "It was a tonic to find oneself again in the free air of good comradeship, cooperation and good humoured stoicism of the front line after months of jealousies and petty rivalries so rampant further back . . . The Company looked a truly amazing sight as they marched into our area. They were loaded down with the usual impediment of ammunition, guns, picks and shovels, but in addition every man had some personal treasure; some had hurricane lamps, some oil house lamps, or an odd oil stove, others carried blankets and baskets and two sections arrived each with a joint of pig they had killed the day before, slung across their haversacks. They looked a motley crew in their camouflage jackets, scarves and weather beaten faces."

As Brigadier Essame of the 43rd Division wrote after the war of the spirit of these men fighting their way to the Rhine: "To subsequent generations accustomed to soft beds, security and elaborate food, it may seem strange to describe Horrocks' command in the Reichswald as a happy Corps. In fact a messtin of hot stew washed down with tea with a tot of rum in it in darkness and rain, gave many a soldier greater pleasure than a banquet in later years. He slept more blissfully when he had the chance in the tail of a truck or on the stone floor of a cellar in his clothes than often later in a heated bedroom in a luxury hotel. Such is the perversity of man that the prospect of ceasing to be alive in the near future adds to the flavour of living at the moment." Essame added, "the good soldier who has stood the test of battle carries with him an unspoken feeling of moral superiority over those who lack his experience, which he retains for the rest of his life."

On 23 February, the key Reichswald town of Calcar surrendered. It had been bitterly fought for and Horrocks, the Corps Commander, felt he had to send a personal message of congratulations to his weary, mud-caked troops. To him the fall of Calcar symbolized that the Battle of the Reichswald was about over.

Still here and there the German paras fought on stubbornly. At Blijenbeek Castle, for instance, the infantry of the 52nd Lowland Division had to launch a full-scale assault across the medieval castle's moat. Three times the paras defending the castle threw the Jocks back. One company of the Lowland infantry was cut down, every last man, as they tried to scale the walls. In the end the castle finally fell when the RAF dropped nine 1,000 lb bombs on the place. Blackened and bewildered the garrison surrendered – *exactly fifteen German paratroopers*!

Soon afterwards, the Germans' last bastion on that sector of the west bank of the Rhine, Xanten, the old Roman fortress, was abandoned by the retreating Germans. Those paras who now found themselves on the wrong side of the great river surrendered to the British. As they marched back to the cages, dirty, ragged and exhausted, Brigadier Essame did something for which he was later criticized by the British press. He called his staff to attention, as the paras straggled past, while he personally saluted the German paras whom he described as "very gallant men".

Now it was almost all over, the victorious infantry rested, drank, looted. John Prebble, the novelist, recalls entering wrecked Xanten to find: "The streets were strewn with rubble . . . men, dusty, sweating, grinning; men with their arms and blouses full of jars of preserved fruits; mattresses, bedding, wireless sets and clothes were everywhere. Canadians, Scots infantrymen, and support troops were moving methodically from house to house . . . amid the wrenching of wood, the cracking of glass, shouts and jeers. There were no civilians anywhere."

It was their time out of war. Mostly they were kids, doomed to lead short, brutish lives which, sooner of later, would be terminated violently. So they wrecked and looted, as long as there weren't any "redcaps" around. They paraded down the rubble-littered streets in stolen top hats, thinking it was a great joke in the manner of school children. They pushed the strange basket-like German prams, filled with looted preserves. If they were Canadians they got drunk, drinking the fierce German *Korn* straight from the stone bottles. If there had been women . . . but there weren't.

To some neutral observer their conduct would have seemed outrageous, but "some neutral observer" could not have visualized in his wildest of dreams the kind of horrors they had seen and endured. War Correspondent Captain R.V. Thompson, that sensitive correspondent for the *Sunday Times*, who always felt a "kind of wonder" and "sense of despair", every time he saw British infantry going up for yet another attack, decided to find out what a batch of new young infantry replacements thought of the mass destruction all around them in the freshly captured town of Udem. It didn't take him long to find out. Suddenly he was confronted by the sight of plate after plate being thrown out of a shattered window. A young soldier put his head out and explained. "The washing up, sir . . . You just chuck it out of the window."

Thompson shook his head sadly. Nothing had any value any more, he told himself.

But a little later standing with a gunner, the bespectacled newspaper correspondent watched yet another company of fresh-faced boys, laden like pack animals and commanded by a teenage subaltern, going up. Some of them would be dead or wounded within the hour, he knew, but still they plodded on down the ruined street. After they had vanished, the gunner turned to Thompson and said thoughtfully, "Compared with them, it's a picnic for the rest of us . . . They're the bloody heroes."

MARCH

"We are going to bounce the Rhine."

Field Marshal Montgomery

I

On Thursday, 1 March General Patton was in a jubilant mood. His troops had just entered Trier, that ancient city founded by the Romans. He had captured his first major German city! Despite the opposition of Eisenhower's top brass to the attack, he had done it behind their backs. Now he signalled Eisenhower's HQ, "Have taken Trier with two divisions. What do you want me to do? Give it back?"

But there was more to his triumph than that. The gate to the Moselle had been opened. Now he had two options. Either he could fight his way up the Moselle to Koblenz and cross the Rhine there. Or he could turn south-east, advance *behind* the Siegfried Line, still holding up the hapless US Seventh Army in the Saar, head for Mainz and cross the Rhine there. Either way he would beat the "little fart" Montgomery. For he was not scheduled to cross the river in his great set-piece crossing for another three weeks yet.

In the end he decided on both options. First he would attack across the River Kyll, which flowed into the Moselle. Once the Kyll had been successfully assaulted by his 5th Infantry Division, his favourite armoured formation, the 4th Armored, would break out of the bridge and go straight for the Rhine to the general area of Andernach.

That night, as the guns on the Kyll started to rumble, Patton returned to his HQ in Luxembourg City and split a bottle of bourbon with his nephew, Fred Ayer. In an expansive mood Patton offered his young nephew some insight into his personal psychology. "In any war," he lectured, "a commander, no matter what his rank, has to send to sure death, a certain number of his men. Some are his personal friends. Any man with a heart would like to sit down and bawl, but he can't. So he sticks out his jaw and swaggers and swears."

As the level of the bourbon got lower and lower, Patton launched into current politics (he had already astonished his staff by maintaining that Eisenhower was already running for president – "he's got the presidential bug"). "We've got a President," he maintained, "who's a great politician . . . But goddamm, the man has never read history! He doesn't understand the Russians and never will. From Genghis Khan to Stalin they haven't changed. They never will and we, we'll never learn until it's too damned late." It was clear that Patton was thinking the unthinkable: soon there would have to be a confrontation with the erstwhile ally, Russia.

"There's another thing people in our government can't understand," he continued. "They can't understand the Germans. It's either that or they're too much influenced by the Jews. Look at this fool unconditional surrender announcement. If the Hun ever needed a burr under his saddle, that's it. He'll now fight like the devil because he'll be ordered to do so."

Having broken with all the conventional wisdoms and sentiments of the time – the things that his troops thought they were fighting for – Patton now turned his full rancour on the politicians. "They'll wear their country's flag in public, but they'll use it to wipe their behinds in the caucus room, if they think it will win them a vote."

But not even Patton's bitter dislike of the men who were running his country, couldn't spoil this day for him. "Now," he proclaimed, "there's almost nothing to stop me. We have fresh divisions arriving. We've mastered the air. We have the best weapons in the world (which wasn't true – in virtually every area the Germans had superior weapons and superior tanks). "We can soon march into Berlin, Vienna, Prague and Belgrade with people throwing flowers in our path."

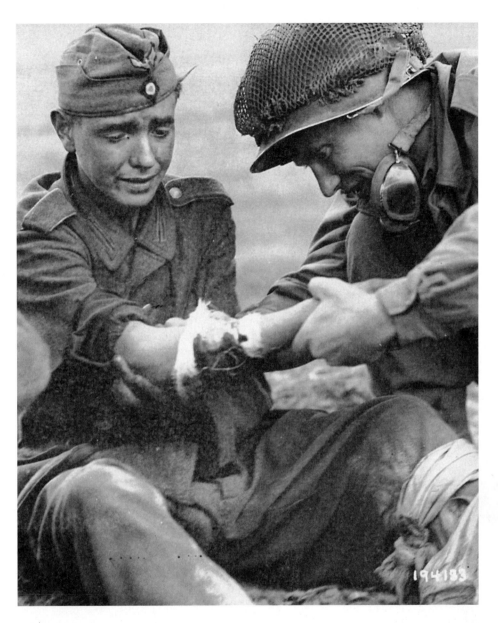

1. Defeat and despair. A US medic helps a wounded German.

2. A member of 6th Airborne clearing a burning farmhouse after the Rhine crossings.

3. German propaganda aimed at splitting the US-UK allies.

4. A sniper uses a tank as protection as he fires on the enemy.

5. A close shave.

6. The capture of Lübeck by the 5th Division led to the surrender of hundreds of Germans.

7. Street fighting.

8. The remains of Hitler's mountain home.

9. The great Nazi survivor – Goering.

10. Relief for Patton as he reaches the Rhine.

11. Link up between the British 51st Highland Division and the US 84th Division, La Roche, January 1945.

12. The British in the Battle of the Bulge, January 1945. Machine gunners of the 51st Division in action.

13. Tank men of the 11th Armoured Division awaiting orders to move into battle – most are boys.

14. Fresh troops move up to the Rhine.

15. The Moyland Schloss, one of the historic Rhine castles, has been captured by Canadian troops during their advance at Moyland, near Calcar.

16. The ultimate weapon. Crocodile flame-thrower tank in action, widely used for house clearance in street fighting.

17 & 18. The reason for German fanatical last-ditch defence: the civilian victims of the great air raids.

19. The men of 6th Airborne on the road to Wismer to prevent the Russians entering West Germany and Denmark pause to view a dead German civilian who attempted to shoot a British sentry.

20. The victors. The men of the Wiltshire Regiment who have just captured a German command post.

21. The Brussels Standard marches past.

22. The author where it all started: Stolzemburg, where US troops first crossed into Germany, 11 September 1944.

But it was not to be. While Patton's young men were already dying once more for strategic objectives which would never be achieved, their commander's wilful and independent strategy would ensure that the bulk of the US Army would swing south-east to fight battles that had no importance or bearing on the conclusion of the war. There would be no triumph march through Berlin and the capitals of central Europe "with people throwing flowers in our path". All the young men's youthful courage, effort and sacrifice would be in vain. One tyranny would be defeated admittedly, but another would replace it for over four decades. The actions and decisions that drunken, grey-haired old man made that March would help to change the course of history in central Europe. Not, however, in the way the great mass of the people in the Western world had hoped for.

But now it was three o'clock in the morning. The bottle of bourbon was empty. "Uncle George" ground out his last cigar and rose easily to his feet. "And now by God we can go to bed," he growled." See you at breakfast."

That day, George S. Patton had enjoyed his last great triumph. Soon his bitter decline would commence. His death in exactly nine months' time must have come as a great release . . .

On that Thursday the German Army was beaten. Unfortunately it did not know it. That day the one-eyed SS General Paul "Papa" Hausser commanding the last section of the *Westwall* in German hands in the Saar area, warned his superiors that since Patton had captured Trier, "the envelopment and annihilation of the Army will be imminent."

"Smiling Albert" Kesselring (so called because he always seemed to be smiling and showing his tombstone-like teeth), now in overall command in the west, took little notice of the SS General's comment. So Hausser stayed in place instead of withdrawing while there was still time and the men of the US Seventh Army who, of course, knew nothing of this, prepared to attack that formidable position upon which the British had been going to "hang out their washing, mother dear", six long years before.

On the following Friday morning, the Americans of the Seventh's 70th Infantry Division stared from the heights on the French side of the border down into the basin of the Saar below. To Lieutenant Colonel Wallace Cheeves, commanding one of the division's infantry battalions, the valley looked "like a picture of peace and contentment". In fact, it was the "front yard of hell". "We weren't just attacking another town, we were cracking the strongest net of fortifications ever constructed by the human race."

All afternoon the rumours went from foxhole to foxhole during the lulls in the enemy mortar fire. They were going into the attack. This was it! It certainly was.

At eight o'clock on the cool clear morning of 3 March, while the artillery pounded the fortifications, the infantry swarmed into the fields, feeling alone and very vulnerable. The machine-gunners were out in front supporting the leading platoon," Sergeant Boughton recalled later. "We were trying to work forward to positions where we could button up the pillbox. Lieutenant Rytting was up forward on reconnaissance, crawling around, through mines as calmly as though he was walking through a potato field back home in Idaho. War was a game to 'Riddle' as we called him. To him the only way to win was to get in the thick of it and play hard . . . That's what he was doing when he went after the pillbox. He went up so close that he got down on his hands and knees and started crawling. He hadn't gone very far when the ground seemed to open up under him. We saw his leg go flying through the air and his whole body leap up and then roll on the ground. The shock and pain almost paralyzed him. He never lost consciousness though. He just lay quietly on the ground and waited for the stretcher-bearers to pick him up."

In the end the medics came up and put the dying officer on

their stretcher. "You guys take it easy," he whispered faintly and then he was gone. His men never saw 'Riddle' again.

There were many "Riddles" that day. For it was the junior leaders, the young "shavetail looies" and "buck sergeants" who bore the brunt of the action, fighting against an enemy hidden in his concrete pillbox or in the cellar of house which had been turned into a mini-fortress.

A company under the command of Lieutenant Wilson attacked through murderous shellfire. They were armed with flame-throwers and white phosphorous grenades. Once they paused, fearful to go on against such fire. Wilson would have none of it. He called to his second in command, Lieutenant Beck, "Beck, this is costing us lives! We'd better keep moving!"

They pushed on through some trees. Mortar bombs started falling all around them. Beck was hit by a fist-sized piece of red-hot shrapnel. It set off the phosphorous grenade on his belt. It erupted into brilliant glowing flame. Beck's whole body was wreathed in that all-consuming fire. But Wilson had no time for Beck and the others who had been hit. He had to push on.

"I emptied my medical pouches that day," Corporal Jimmie Owen, a medic, recalled later. "I tried to take care of the worst cases first, but there were so many I hardly knew which ones needed help most. I got a line of walking wounded started back up the hill to the aid station. The casualty-collecting point was in the edge of a wood clear at the top of a ridge. About two trips up that hill with a litter was all a guy could stand."

Many straggled back of their own accord. Their faces were blanched with shock, eyes wild and staring. Some trembled. Some mumbled meaningless sounds. Others stared down at their torn limbs as if outraged. Why should this have happened to them? Some accepted their hurt bravely. Medic Monroe Gable recalled meeting Master Sergeant Lewis Ripley staggering up that steep hill. He had "a crude bandage wrapped around a hole as big as an egg in his elbow. His face was ashen grey and he could hardly walk. But he refused to let me give him first aid or a shot of morphine. He told me to help the other boys first."

And still the fighting went on. Up front, Lieutenant Wilson's company was clearing out a line of workers' houses. Suddenly in the nearest house the Germans put out a white flag. They wanted to surrender. As Pfc Corrigan, one of Wilson's company, recalled, "When the guys saw it, they only got sore. Everyone was for moving in and cleaning them out."

Wilson would have none of it. He was from West Point and did everything by the book. Behind his back his men called him "little boy blue" because of his prissy West Point attitude to everything. So the Germans were saved and the "Trailblazers", as the men of the 70th Division were called, pushed on to attack the next house. Suddenly two shots rang out. A sergeant went down blood pouring from his nose and mouth. For a few moments the attackers were puzzled. Where was the fire coming from? Then they spotted it. A small pillbox built into the side of the house. It would be a tricky position to attack.

Wilson, always the leader, decided he'd try to get a better look at the little pillbox. He clambered up the debris-littered stairs of a house the company had just taken, accompanied by two other soldiers. There he spotted a group of his unsuspecting men attempting to dig in right under the sights of the hidden sniper. Ignoring the danger to himself he leant out of the window and shouted at them to run for cover.

Suddenly he jerked. He staggered back from the shattered window. "My God, I'm hit," he gasped, his voice full of disbelief. Abruptly he thrust out his legs, as if attempting to brace himself in a last desperate attempt to fight off Death. "Slap my face!" he commanded. *"Slap my face!"*

A soldier dropped his rifle and struck him across the cheek. To no avail. Wilson dropped to the floor. With one last bout of energy, he slammed his boots against a heavy oaken table. It slithered right across the room. Then he moved no more.

"When I went upstairs," Corrigan remembered after the war, "it was all over. I opened his shirt and found two small holes just above his heart. There was not a trace of blood on the outside. He must have bled internally. I realized that sooner or later he would have been killed, but now that it had happened none of us could quite believe it. I took the codes and overlays out of his pocket and looked at his AGO card. He was only twenty-one and as he lay there he didn't look anywhere near that. His hair was cropped close and he had no beard at all. He was just a kid, yet he proved himself to be the driving factor of the whole company. He was everything that could be expected of an officer and soldier. When he died the spirit of the company died with him."

There were lots like Lieutenant Wilson, whose men had ridiculed him as "little boy blue", that grim March day.

II

"The soldier who won't fuck," Patton had once exclaimed in a moment of tipsy exuberance, "won't fight". Patton who had three mistresses during the course of his fighting career in North Africa and Europe certainly knew what he was talking about. And that statement was one that the men would have supported wholeheartedly. Now for the first time, his soldiers and those of all the other Allied armies, were crossing into Germany in their thousands to find villages and towns, decked with white flags, towels, grandpa's long johns – anything that betokened surrender – and inhabited by children, old men – *and women*!

But for the sex-starved young men, there was one large catch. These were *enemy* women and officially they were not allowed even to talk to them, never mind anything else.

On the first day of that March, the Supreme Commander, General Eisenhower, had made the position quite clear. In a printed folder to be handed out to every Allied soldier, he stated: "You are entering Germany not as a liberator but as a victor. Do not keep smiling. Never offer a cigarette . . . nor offer him your hand. Germans will respect you as long as they see you as a successor to Hitler, who never offered them *his* hand . . . Distrust everybody . . . Never give way. Anything that is granted as a favour will be regarded by the Germans as his right and he will subsequently demand twice as much. He thinks fair play is cowardice. The only way to get along with the Germans is to make them respect you, to make them feel the hand of the master."

The concept of "non-fraternization" had been born. Immediately the young soldiers termed German womanhood as "frat" and the pursuit of the "frowleins", inspite of the fact that anyone caught with them could be fined or even jailed, was named "fratting."

In the US Army a soldier seen "fratting" could be fined up to sixty-five dollars, but as the US Army newspaper *Stars and Stripes* noted five days later, "There are soldiers who don't care – non-fraternization is just a brass-imposed doctrine, they say . . . For officers and men in these categories, and though a minority, they are a considerable one – the current situation is a natural for fraternization. There are a great many Germans around. At the moment they are friendly and the soldiers are lonely."

The *Stars and Stripes* had assessed the situation correctly. With the top brass feverishly preparing for the crossing of the Rhine, passes to the fleshpots of Paris, Brussels and Biarritz were few and far between. Young men, whose lives might end abruptly very soon, wanted sex and they were going to have it whatever "Ike" stated to the contrary.

Living cheek-by-jowl with German women in villages and hamlets, where control by superior officers was hard to maintain, the men took no notice of the "frat ban", especially when they had been drinking. There were cases of rape, attempted rape and sexual molestations. By March the US Army alone was recording 500 cases monthly and they would increase.

Of course, it wasn't all one-sided. There were plenty of *Veronika Danke schöns* (Veronica Thankyous) about. They were easily available for a can of coffee or a bar of chocolate, which most of them had not seen for years. Many a young soldier lost his virginity to these amateur whores that spring. But these *Veronika Danke schöns*, brought up in the easy lax morality of the war years with most of their menfolk away for years on end at the front, sometimes had more to offer the *Tommies* and *Amis* than their bodies. They often left behind a little "souvenir" of the swift brutal coupling in a barn, down some cellar, or, in some cases, in the gutter. After all, their nickname could be shortened to represent that scourge which would sweep through the Allied armies in Germany by the summer – VD!

Already by March hundreds of men were being sent back to the "pox hospitals" suffering from "clap" or "siff". If they were afflicted by both, as some poor unfortunates were, then, in the parlance of the British, they'd got the "full house".

The VD sufferer's plight was unenviable. He would be treated harshly by both doctors and sisters, who felt these men were wasting their time. The patient would be pumped full of the new wonder drug, penicillin, a shot every three hours, day and night for two to four days. Then he would be subjected to the dreaded "umbrella": a razor-sharp catheter inserted into his scrotum to clear away any possible lesions. Thereafter, as the patients moaned, "I pissed blood and muck ten different ways!"

Already in the autumn, the US Army was sending 600 men daily to the VD hospitals and the figures for the British and Canadian Armies could not have been much less. By the end of the campaign, it was estimated that the US Army had lost over a quarter of a million man-hours due to VD and that the VD rate was running to forty-two cases per thousand GIs. In the end Eisenhower issued a warning that any German woman knowingly giving VD to an Allied soldier could be punished by death.

The dire warning had no effect whatsoever. The "fratting" went on.

With the Allied armies closing up to the Rhine everywhere (save in the Saar where the bitter fighting still continued) and the soldiers relaxed, the staff officers at Montgomery's HQ worked feverishly to complete the plan for the "Master's" great assault on the Rhine. As Montgomery saw it, Eisenhower had approved a crossing of the Rhine in two areas. His own armies would "bounce the Rhine", as he phrased it, in the north between Emmerich and Wesel and Bradley's armies would do the same between Mainz and Karlsruhe. But the "Master" knew that his own operation would be the more important. The Mainz–Karlsruhe crossing led to the unimportant south of Germany.

His crossing on the other hand, went straight into the Ruhr, the centre of Germany's industrial might, and from thence to the capital, Berlin. With 27 divisions under his command, including those of General Simpson's Ninth Army, he was quite sure that once the Rhine was crossed he "could crack about the plains of Northern Germany, chasing the enemy from pillar to post".

But in that first week of March, something happened to change the whole balance of Allied strategy. On 7 March, the railway bridge at Remagen across the Rhine was captured by Lieutenant Karl Timmermann with a company of tanks of the US 9th Armored Division. For that week, that railway bridge became the "most famous bridge in the world". When Alan Moorehead, the Australian war correspondent, heard the news further up the Rhine at Cologne that afternoon, he called it "the most romantic story of the campaign". But ironically the man who had led that bold and dangerous charge across the bridge at Remagen was born less than a hundred miles away as the son of an American deserter from the US Army of Occupation after the Great War and his German bride. Indeed Timmermann didn't speak English till his father returned with the family when he was three years old and he always maintained he only joined the US Army because trashcan lids "froze up one winter in Nebraska and I had nothing to eat".

But no one mentioned Timmermann's German origins now. The officer who had been born "on the wrong side of the tracks" was fêted and the news of his captured bridge was immediately signalled to General Hodges, the commander of the US First

Army to which the 9th Armored belonged. He, in his turn, immediately telephoned his superior, Bradley, and told him the startling news.

"A *bridge*? You mean you've got one intact on the Rhine?" Bradley exclaimed in delight.

Hodges assured Bradley he had and Bradley said, "Hot dog, Courtney, this will bust him wide open! Are you getting the stuff across?"

"I'm giving it everything I've got," Hodges replied, realizing already that Bradley, his boss, was not going to stick to the agreed strategy.

"Shove everything you can across it, Courtney," Bradley said urgently, "and button the bridgehead up tightly."

Now the Army Group Commander was committed. But he still hadn't Eisenhower's permission for the new bridgehead. That night Ike's operations officer was his guest at dinner. The latter told Bradley bluntly, "You're not going anywhere down there at Remagen," which was very true. The terrain was wooded, hilly and difficult and the road network was poor. "Besides, it just doesn't fit into the overall plan."

Bradley exploded, *"Plan*, hell! A bridge is a bridge and mighty damn good *anywhere* across the Rhine."

In the end Bradley informed Eisenhower, who was at a dinner party at his HQ at Rheims. According to one present, Eisenhower was delighted at Bradley's news. "Brad, that's wonderful," he exclaimed. "Sure, get right on across with everything you've got. It's the best break we've had . . . To hell with the planners."

Another guest at the dinner, General "Gentleman Jim" Gavin, commander of the US 82nd Airborne Division, who rather liked Montgomery (he was one of the few US generals who did), realized immediately what was happening. "The seizure of the crossing at Remagen," he wrote many years later, "suggested to General Bradley . . . a 'Bradley Plan' that envisioned a direct thrust to the east to link up with the Soviets.

"This would obviate the need to give American divisions to Montgomery and would relegate Montgomery and his Army Group to a secondary role.

"The capture of the Remagen bridge and Eisenhower's prompt decision to exploit the crossing was a historic event of extraordinary importance. It would allow General Eisenhower to give free rein to his own generals, Bradley, Patton, Hodges and Simpson. But for it to be carried out successfully it was important that the details of the plan should *not* be disclosed to the British until it was accomplished."

The decision to relegate Montgomery's armies to what amounted to a flank guard for Bradley's main thrust after the Rhine was crossed symbolized what had happened to the Anglo-American alliance since D-Day.

Although Churchill had felt in April 1944 that he was being forced into the cross-Channel landing "by the Russians and by the United States military authorities", it had been the British who had been the leaders of the great invasion of Europe. They had been in charge of the land, air and naval attack. They had shown tremendous national competence in espionage, deception, technical innovation and professionalism. Without Britain as a base, British leadership and knowhow, the Americans would not have been able to launch the invasion in June 1944. Even three-quarters of the shipping which transported them and the other allies across the Channel, was British.

But as American military power and experience grew, with three Americans fighting for every one of Montgomery's men, the American generals' demands for the kudos and glory of the great victories grew and grew. In 1944 they had seen the British generals as the true professionals who had been hardened by five years of war. One year later they saw them as bumbling, cautious old fogeys, who were too set in their ways to understand modern, mobile, fast-moving warfare, as they felt they did.

But it went further than that. On the greater political scene America was emerging as the future world superpower. A series of international conferences held in the States in the course of 1944, on American initiative and with American agendas, laid the foundation for the post-war world. It was clear that America was already the dominant partner in the "Big Three" of America, Russia and Britain. Already Henry R. Luce, the founder of *Time* magazine, was hailing "The American Century".

Now, still in secret, the American generals wanted to ensure that Montgomery learned that hard fact of life. Let him have his one last battle, the final hurrah of the "Victor of El Alamein". Thereafter, he would be relegated to the shadows and the world would see *American* soldiers led by *American* generals winning World War Two.

But while the generals schemed and plotted, the PBI still fought and died. In that second week of March, the infantry of the US Seventh Army, with the 70th and 63rd Infantry Divisions in the lead, were still battling their way across the River Saar and through the Siegfried Line fortifications beyond.

The top brass had told the fighting troops that the pillboxes were held by "retreads" from the German *Luftwaffe*, who knew nothing about ground warfare. That hadn't reassured the infantry. As Lieutenant Chappel of the 70th Division commented later: "It made no difference whether they knew anything about infantry tactics or not. All they had to do was to sit inside the thick concrete bunkers and pull the trigger of a machine-gun. It was sure suicide to cross the fields swept by perfect enemy fire, but orders were orders and we were going to try it."

"My platoon jumped off first, "recalled Sergeant Rysso afterwards. "I had two squads forward and one back. As soon as we started to move, the Krauts threw over a lot of artillery and mortars, but most of it fell in back of us. Pfc Condict was the first man over the knob of the hill in front of the line. When he came back he was sweating and his face was pale. "It's going to be rough,' was all he said. We kept going until the two leading platoons were at the top of the hill. We could all see the dragons teeth, pillboxes, dugouts and trenches from there. The hill was completely bare and we stood out in plain sight like sore thumbs. The Krauts couldn't help but see us. They waited until we were out on the flat ground and then cut loose."

Suddenly, startlingly, the enemy opened up with their machine-guns and mortars. Tracer zipped towards the advancing Americans in lethal profusion. Man after man went down groaning, some dead before they hit the ground. The Germans even fired at the manure heaps which were everywhere in case the *Amis* were attempting to hide behind them. The stalled company commanders called for artillery. But the shells bounced off the thick concrete hide of the pillboxes like glowing ping-pong balls. Tanks were sent up. One of the Shermans turned tail immediately when it breasted the hill and saw the line of deadly bunkers below. But the rest kept on doggedly. For a few minutes they slogged it out with the pillboxes, shells bursting all around them. Then the tank commanders lost their nerve. They started to retreat, telling the stalled infantry that the ground was too soft for tanks.

Sergeant Rysso ordered the survivors of his group to take cover. "Once we had reached temporary safety, I started to reorganize the men we had left," he recalled after the war. "Dunn made two attempts to go out into the field to get the wounded, but was driven back by machine-gun fire. Then Newton, the medic, went out accompanied by Penland, Dunn, Boering and Mann. Strange to say they drew no fire, even though they were plainly visible to the Germans. They found Palmer dead, Castro with a broken leg and Jannick unconscious with a hole in his head . . . Cuervo and Condict were also lying on the ground badly wounded. Newton did what he could for the men. He gave them all a shot of morphine and then waited for the litter bearers to come up."

What happened to Sergeant Rysso's platoon, a series of personal little tragedies, was happening to similar platoons of the two assault divisions everywhere that March day. The Germans were fighting back hard from their fortifications though there were rumours among the defenders that the *Amis* had crossed the Moselle and were heading for the Rhine. Still they fought on and the wounded lay everywhere in the open fields waiting for succour.

Sergeant Penland, lying out in no-man's land, wounded, recalled afterwards, "Out of the corner of my eye, I saw two men supporting a third coming toward the shell crater (in which he was sheltering). I glanced about and recognized Andrews on the right, supporting Darling who had been wounded in the right thigh. I just got out the first word of warning, 'Get down!' when a large calibre shell screamed over very low and hit directly on the three men. I saw a tremendous flash of flame and a fearful cloud of black smoke. Pieces of men's bodies came flying through the air. The concussion blew off my helmet and threw me to the bottom of the crater which was filled with mud and water. One man's horribly torn body flew over my head and hit the water beside me. Newton was standing next to me nearest the shell and was blown into the water. I grabbed him to keep him from sinking under. He was covered with blood from the men who had been hit. I asked him if he had been hit. He said he didn't know and crawled to help another man who was pushing himself toward the water with only his legs. I looked around and saw just a man's chest and hands sticking out of the water. I grabbed to pull him out, thinking possibly he might still be alive and was drowning. When I got him out though, I saw he was mangled and dead so I let him slip back into the water."

As Pfc Hy Schorr, a 29-year old machine-gunner with the 70th Infantry, who would win three Bronze Stars in the campaign, remembered long afterwards: "By now most of the guys in my machine-gun section had been hit, wounded or killed, or had been evacuated with combat fatigue. For three months the Division had been taking terrific casualties, but still they kept us at it, plugging at that goddam Siegfried Line."

But behind the *Westwall*, the German front was crumbling rapidly, as Patton's Third Army dashed for the Rhine at half a dozen spots. Indeed the enemy retreat was swiftly turning into a rout. General Ferber, commanding the German Seventh Army which was defending the area, found himself reduced to directing what was left of his shattered army from a local post office, using the civilian telephone network as his sole means of communication.

Now Patton's tankers, urged on frantically by "Ole Blood an' Guts," were racing forward at twenty-five miles a day. In a letter home to his wife that month, Lieutenant Fishler of the US 4th Armored wrote: "No German village is complete without a full set of white flags, although they are generally impromptu affairs, such as tablecloths, napkins, shirts and grandpa's long winter underpants. If there are some German soldiers to contest our entrance, the reception is a little different at first, although later it amounts to the same thing, except the white flags fly from the rubble."

For Patton and his men, as they drove to the Rhine, this was "Patton's Third Army Memorial" technique. If a village or town resisted, then it was plastered with artillery fire until it surrendered. Then, as Patton reasoned, the place would be a semi-permanent memorial to the fact that he and his army had passed this way.

Koblenz fell. Medic Atwell described the chaos of the city's last few hours. "Infantrymen who had been in the cellars ran past drunkenly firing anywhere and shrill, over-excited German girls, impatient for rape, ran after them through the shells and falling rubble. A French newspaper photographer drove up in a jeep, brandished a revolver and staggered on drunk to take pictures. Somebody played "Lili Marlene" on a piano. The Frenchman wanted to shoot somebody. In a living room drunken American soldiers bumped into drunken German soldiers, all armed, with 'excuse me . . . pardon me.'

"Don Stoddard (a comrade) dashed into the street during a barrage and came across one of his men having sexual intercourse with a woman. Long streams of German prisoners came by guarded by drunken Americans. Many of the prisoners were drunk themselves, their waterbottles filled with cognac."

Germany on the west bank of the Rhine was falling apart. Drunken soldiers, freed slave workers, raping and looting, the merciless pounding of villages and towns into surrender, the heartless, pointless shooting of prisoners in cold blood – they were all part of the general chaos and confusion.

Despite the confusion and chaos, Patton brooked no delay. Time was running out fast. Now Patton was here, there and everywhere, urging his men to ever greater efforts, chewing out corps commanders if they were too slow, sacking generals for not being aggressive enough, threatening enlisted men.

Once he discovered that replacement tanks were not reaching his fighting divisions quickly enough, he made his own personal survey. He discovered the huge tank transporters laid up in small towns and villages and concluded that their drivers were "whooping it up with the local damery". Angrily Patton ordered that every sergeant commanding a tank transporter should "be busted to buck private". It worked. The fighting regiments received their replacement tanks on time thereafter.

And then, at last, there it was – *the Rhine*!

"We've got to get a bridgehead at once," Patton told his staff excitedly when he heard the news. "The enemy is in chaos on our front. But if we delay seventy-two hours he'll reorganize and we'll have to fight to push him out of our way. We must not give him that chance, regardless of what political machinations are going on up above. We destroyed two armies in one week with a handful of losses to ourselves and I don't propose to give the bastards a chance to reorganize."

Flashing a quick smile at his admiring staff, he added, "We're going to make a crossing at once, I don't care how or where we get the necessary equipment, but it must be got. Steal it, beg it or make it. But I want it and it had better be there where we need it when we need it." He pointed his big cigar at them like an offensive weapon. "We're going to cross the Rhine and we're going to do it before I'm a day older!"

On the morning of 23 March, early on, an excited Patton called Bradley and said, "Brad, don't tell anyone but I'm across!"

"Well, I'll be damned!" Bradley exclaimed. "You mean the Rhine?"

"Sure I am. I sneaked a division over last night. But there are so few Krauts around there that they don't know it yet. So don't make any announcement – we'll keep it secret till we see how it goes."

But Patton was not one to hide his light under a bushel. That night, he telephoned Bradley again and yelled, "Brad, for God's sake tell the world we're across! We knocked down thirty-three Krauts today when they came after our pontoon bridges. I want the world to know that the Third Army made it before Monty starts across."

But the "world" already knew. At that morning's press briefing at Bradley's HQ, the representative of Patton's Third Army had announced: "Without benefit of aerial bombing, ground smoke, artillery preparation and airborne assistance, the Third Army at 2200 hours, Thursday evening, March 22, crossed the Rhine river."

The dig was obvious. It was aimed at Montgomery. He would be crossing twenty-three hours later with all the aerial, artillery, airborne assistance the Third Army's representative had detailed. Maliciously Patton was twisting the knife in the wound. The "little fart" had it coming.

III

On the night of 23 March, the great bombardment began. Along a 22-mile length of the Rhine, Montgomery's men opened up with 3,500 guns, supported by 2,000 anti-aircraft cannon, many thousands of mortars and scores of "mattresses", rocket launchers massed in batteries. For three long hours now the artillery would blast the German positions on the opposite bank. "The softening up" process had commenced.

"The noise was so terrific," the historian of the Lincolns wrote, that "conversation in Battalion Headquarters was almost impossible."

"Our targets were pre-selected," R. Saunders of the 103rd Regiment, Royal Artillery observed, "and the guns lost the paint from their barrels." Captain Wilson, waiting to cross with his troop of "crocodiles", flame-throwing tanks, noted, "East and west, as far as I could see, the night was lit by gunfire; it flickered through the trees and flashed on the underside of the clouds. The ground shook ceaselessly and now and again there was a violent continuous explosion like a pack of cards being snapped."

The order was given for the assault infantry to clamber into their Buffaloes for the assault crossing. Most of them, Canadian, British and American, were nervous. They knew that the Germans would fight like devils to hold the Rhine. For nothing could save the Fatherland once the Rhine line fell. They told jokes, "which no one would have laughed at ordinarily," Captain Wilson noted, "wandering off frequently to the latrine". That was a sure sign of funk.

At precisely nine o'clock on that perfect moonlit night, the first Buffaloes waddled into the water like great metal ducks. In the lead were the 7th Battalion, the Black Watch, the 7th Argylls, followed by the 1st Battalion, the Black Watch, all from the 51st Highland Division. Five years before, the old 51st had surrendered to the Germans at St Valery. Now the wheel had come the full circle. They were about to deal a death blow to the Germans. Four minutes later an anxious General Horrocks, their Corps Commander, received the message he was waiting for: *"The Black Watch have landed safely on the far bank."*

At ten o'clock it was the turn of the 1st Commando Brigade. War correspondent R.V. Thompson was there as they moved. He wrote later in the *Sunday Times*: "Never have I seen troops so magnificently confident. The back of the Buffalo closed. Without pause the amphibious tank roared over the dyke and within two minutes crunched down into the Rhine. Overhead the perfect sky was filled with vast red sheaves of tracer poured from Bofors and the harsh muttering of massed machine-guns weaving incessantly under the whiplash of the heavier guns."

In one Buffalo there was Corporal Cosgrave. He was a veteran of the Normandy fighting where he'd often gone hungry. This time he was determined he'd eat on the other side. Somewhere he had "liberated" what he thought was a drake, which he'd named Hector. Now Hector was tied to his pack squawking his head off with fright. "Shut the fucking thing up, Corp," the other commandos cried repeatedly. "It's driving us barmy." In the end Cosgrave sealed Hector's beak up with tape. Thus, in, at least, *canard* silence, the Buffalo ploughed to the other side.

Corporal Barry Pierce was first of the commandos to reach the other side. As the artillery barrage lifted and the first German defenders lifted their heads, Pierce, a Royal Marine, went at them. This was trench warfare, 1915 style. Grenades hissed through the air. Tommy guns chattered. Then Pierce's commandos went in using, in the parlance of that old war, "cold steel". The German resistance crumpled within minutes.

The first Buffalo was hit. It went out of control. Next moment it burst into flame. The burning fuel seared the length of the vehicle like a giant blowtorch. Badly wounded and burnt, Lieutenant William James leapt ashore. A handful of signallers and a forward artillery observer from a mountain battery followed. Together with his little band, he scurried for cover in a large factory which the commandos had selected before the crossing. Now it turned out to be a factory for the manufacture of what is quaintly called "sanitary ware". As Corporal Cosgrave recalled long afterwards, "That night more of the blokes were wounded by splinters of flying shithouses than Jerry bullets."

Now it was ten-thirty. R.V. Thompson looked at his watch. "A day earlier we had been told that an important key town would be 'blotted'. And now deluging down out of the sky an appalling weight of bombs seemed to rip both town and the very earth itself to fragments, and at once a great crimson stain of smoke and flame poured up like an open wound so that the puffs of the bursting flak were crimson too and the river seemed the colour of blood."

It was 250 Lancasters of "Arthur Harris* & Company, House Removers" at work, dropping 1,000 tons of bombs in a very short space of time on the key town of Wesel.

Watching the awesome spectacle from the other side of the river, Australian War Correspondent, Alan Moorehead, recorded: "The Lancasters filled the air with roaring and at last the cataclysmic, unbelievable shock of the strike. Great black stretches of the skyline – buildings and trees and wide acres of city parkland – simply detached themselves from the earth and mounted slowly upwards in the formation of a fountain. As the rubble reached its zenith, it suddenly filled

* Air Marshal Harris, C-in-C of Bomber Command.

with bursting light and a violent wind came tearing across the river."

To commando Major Bertholomew crouched in the "loo" factory, reeling and gasping at the detonations, it seemed "as if more than mortal powers had been unleashed".

That night Wesel died.

Now it was the turn of the 15th Scottish Division to go across. BBC correspondent Wynford Vaughan-Thomas was with them. He described their boats as "racing for that hell on the other side . . . Now we're utterly alone, it seems – right out in the midst of this whirling stream . . . waiting all the time for them to open up as we lie helpless . . ." But they weren't spotted. With a sense of relief they reached the other side unharmed.

Now the CO of the assault party nodded to his piper. This historic moment had to be celebrated in true Scottish fashion. With due ceremony, in spite of the murder and mayhem going on all around, the piper raised the pipes to his lips. He blew hard. Nothing happened! He tried once more. Nothing save an "agonising wail" from the bagpipes. As Thomas reported, "If ever a man was near to tears, it was our piper."

This was to have been his great moment, something he could tell his grandkids about, if he survived. Now he cried in utter despair, "Ma pipes, mon, they'll na play".

In the British sector they were all across, the Jocks, the Canadians, the Commandos. Now it was the turn of the Americans of Simpson's Ninth Army. During the hour-long artillery softening up, the Ninth had fired no less than 65,000 shells. 1,500 bombers had attacked a dozen German airfields just behind the Rhine. But as the Americans of the 30th US Infantry started to cross, German light mortars sprang into action.

Yet nothing could stop "Roosevelt's Butchers", as the 30th believed they were called by the Germans. Their storm boats followed the lines of white tracer which were being used to guide them. Two of the boats were knocked out immediately spilling the men into the fast-flowing current. Minutes later the others ground to a halt on the mud on the other side. The GIs swarmed up the bank and were heading straight for their assembly points with only a few shots fired at them through the swirling dawn mist. As Lieutenant Refvem of the 30th said afterwards, "There was no real fight. The artillery had done the job for us."

Within two hours the 30th Division was firmly established, at a cost of a couple of dozen casualties. It was no different with their running mate, the 79th Division, further down the river. By dawn the division had two regiments across and firmly established. Prisoners told their American captors they had never encountered anything like it (the artillery fire). It completely stunned, scared and shook them.

It was different in the British-Canadian sector. All night the commandos at Wesel had been engaged in the bloody, costly business of house-to-house fighting, working their way through the smoking brick rubble of what was left of the old Rhenish city.

It was fighting of the toughest kind. It demanded skill and strong nerves. Men stalked and killed each other at ranges of less than twenty yards. Even a German general was killed, pistol in hand, in this deadly close quarter fighting.

"One patrol (of Germans)", a commando corporal reported later, "came down the railway line and we waited till we could literally see the whites of their eyes before killing them . . . Later a second section of Germans came across the field . . . we just picked them off like sitting birds. They had no idea where the fire was coming from and simply lay flat on the ground ready to be shot."

Occasionally, however, amidst this cruel house-to-house fighting, where no quarter was given or expected, there were moments of light relief. Dug in among some ruins, Corporal

Cosgrave discovered to his astonishment that "Hector" was not what he was supposed to be – "he should have bloody well been called "Hectorine"! For suddenly the bird laid an egg. As the Corporal didn't like duck eggs and was sick of the bird anyway, the false Hector was given away. He consoled himself he wouldn't starve now, for they had just found a cellar full of pig carcasses. There'd be grub enough for as long as "this little lot" lasted.

Sometimes the humour that night was a little bitter. A captured German colonel was brought to the cellar where the commando commander, Mills-Roberts, had set up his head-quarters. The German was cross-examined and then dismissed. As he turned to leave, he spoke to one of the commandos and said in a lordly manner, "Do you mind carrying my bag for me?"

Mills-Roberts had a short fuse, especially with Germans (one day soon he would hit a German field marshal over the head with his own field marshal's baton). He rounded on the German colonel immediately. "As a member of the master race," he snorted, "you can surely deal with something as small as that?"

Suddenly abashed, the colonel allowed himself to be taken away to the cage. He carried his own bag.

By dawn Montgomery had three bridgeheads well estab-lished, though heavy fighting was going on at all three of them. At Rees in particular, the 51st Highland Division was finding the going "sticky" and General Rennie, its commander, decided to go up and see for himself. Rennie, who had escaped the débâcle of 1940, and who had fought ever since, had been very apprehensive this March. He didn't know why, but he had a feeling that something might go wrong.

He arranged to meet one of his brigadiers to discuss the situation at a crossroads. They did and, the impromptu conference concluded, the familiar figure of the general, in his duffle coat and balmoral bearing the red hackle of the

Black Watch, started to walk back to his jeep. He didn't get far. Suddenly there was a thud and the obscene howl of a mortar being fired. Men of the German 15th Panzer Grenadier Division, an old enemy of the 51st, had spotted the lone jeep. The vehicle took a direct hit. Its back axle collapsed and thick black smoke started to pour from it.

Horrified, an ADC ran to the still figure sprawled out at a grotesque angle in the smoking wreckage. He shook Rennie and asked him stupidly if he was all right. But the General gave no reply.

Minutes later the nearest aid post confirmed the worst – Thomas Rennie was dead.

"Aye, he was a guid general," one of his beloved Jocks remarked later, "He wasna a shoutin' kinda man." But for the time being the Jocks were not going to be told of the death of their commander. Horrocks, Rennie's Corps Commander, who knew that the dead general "had hated everything about it" (the Rhine crossing) hurriedly crossed the river himself. All three brigades of the 51st were engaged in hard fighting so that even another general, one of the three brigadiers, had been wounded, though he remained at his post. He conferred with the three brigadiers and told them that for the moment the rank-and-file should not be told of Rennie's death in action.

The officers of the 5th Seaforths about to go through their toughest action of the whole war were told, "The General's dead. But you mustn't tell anyone yet, not until this business is over." So with heavy hearts they led their Jocks to the slaughter to come. All around shells were bursting and the whole horizon seemed to be burning. Even as they set off down the road, long range guns opened up on them and caused casualties. Doggedly they slogged on.

As soon as they reached their objective, the hamlet of Groin, all hell was let loose. The place was defended by those "bloody para-boys" and they were determined to hold it. The German *Fallschirmjäger* attacked immediately they saw the Seaforths.

106

A Jock platoon was wiped out save for eight men. Another was forced to retreat. The Seaforth's colonel was hit and wounded.

As one of the Jocks, Sgt Goldney, remembered: "It was terrible. All the buildings were on fire. Roofs were caving in and sparks were flying all over the place. Cattle were trapped inside. The stench sickened me. In the firelight I could see both the Boche and my own lads." A Company to which Goldney belonged was about done.

D Company was sent in. Its lead platoon was pinned down almost immediately by the terrific volume of German fire. Most of the fire was coming from one point in the centre of the street. Captain Gardiner asked for volunteers to make a flank attack on the place. Corporal Purchase and five of his friends, who had been together for a long time, volunteered to tackle the place. "We'll do the job properly," the corporal said firmly, "if I have to do it myself."

Lance-Corporal Green, who was one of the little group of volunteers, recalled what happened: "The Boche were only seventy yards away. They weren't fast enough to catch Purchase and Grey when they made a dive for it, but of course they were just waiting for us and whenever we showed ourselves we got a burst throught the hair."

Crouched in a ditch with the bullets flying over his head, Green heard his two comrades shouting, "Give up, you bastards! The Seaforths are here!" A little later there was a burst of spandau fire and silence.

"We knew what that meant. They were our mates and we were all boiled up. 'To hell with this,' Green shouted. 'Come on.'"

They clambered out of the ditch. Purchase and Grey, another volunteer, were lying on the ground near a ditch which held forty-six Germans.

"We were mad when we saw them lying there. We didn't know what we were doing. We stood in the open, and called the Boche all the names in creation and yelled at them to come out. And so help me, they did. A wee white flag came over the edge and then two or three and then the whole issue. Forty-six of them. The officer was one of those right clever baskets – big smiles all over his face.

"Purchase was the best section leader we ever had."

Dawn came for the American combat crews at 0538 British Double Summer Time on 24 March. The orderlies ran from hut to hut in the dozen or so airborne camps scattered across France south of Paris, waking the glider pilots for the great drop. Being American they ate a huge pre-combat breakfast – steak, ice cream and apple pie, washed down with as much "java" as they could drink.

Reveille came for the British paras on the other side of the Channel at 0245. In blacked-out Nissen huts they breakfasted off dried egg and sausage and plenty of "char".

But in both the British and American messes, the men of the 6th Airborne and the US 17th Airborne Divisions, made the same hoary old crack, *The condemned men ate a hearty breakfast.* And it was true. For nearly two thousand young Britons and Americans this *would* be the last breakfast they ever ate.

The British paras took off first. By 0700 that morning, the planes and the gliders were assembling above Hawkinge, Kent, in streams that stretched as far as the eye could see – 429 planes and gliders carrying 4,876 men. Two hours later the Americans took off. Like everything else in Montgomery's grandiose plan for crossing the Rhine, the paradrop would be bigger than D-Day, with 25,000 men, British, Canadian and American, on the high ground on the other side of the Rhine. There they would facilitate the breakout of the ground forces. But one thing the planners had seemed to overlook was that the planes would be flying over "flak alley", the corridor leading to the Ruhr. There the Germans had massed anti-aircraft guns for years and the sixteen-year-old gunners and the female auxiliaries had already been alerted. The Rhine drop could well turn out to be a worse tragedy than Arnhem, the previous September!

By 0800 the two streams, British and American, had rendezvoused just south of Brussels. Now they became the largest single-day airborne operation of the war. The entire sky train now took three hours and twenty minutes to pass any given spot. It was a tremendous undertaking.

As the British gliders flew over Waterloo an officer glider pilot turned to his sergeant pilot and said, "My great-great-grandfather fought at Waterloo." The working-class NCO was not impressed. "So did mine and it was probably your great-great-grandfather that got him killed. Try not to do the same to me today."

That probably apocryphal story was the sign of the times. After being brainwashed for four years with "ABCA" and "Current Affairs" lectures, Michael Foot's *Daily Mirror* with its "soldier rights" and Barbara Castle, "the new Britain", the "Beveridge Plan" and the future "Welfare State", the other ranks had grown a little "bolshie". Soon they'd kick out the old man, Winston Churchill, who made all this possible and who was now waiting on the Rhine to view the greatest battle yet to be fought by the British Army. This would be the last hurrah!

Churchill waited with the Top Brass. He had suffered a series of mishaps getting to the Rhine. He had forgotten his false teeth – they were delivered to him discreetly, wrapped in a handkerchief, by an anxious dispatch rider. He had had his cap knocked off by the gun of an armoured car and he had had some difficulty in finding the VIP latrine. But now he was here. "I should have liked to have deployed my men in redcoats on the plain down there and ordered them to charge," he rumbled. "But now my armies are too vast."

Suddenly there was a "subdued but intense roar", as the Great Man explained it later, "a rumbling of swarms of aircraft." Churchill lurched to his feet and stumbled a few yards down the slope, yelling with delight, *They're coming . . . They're coming!*"

They were indeed. The airborne armada had reached the Rhine.

The slaughter started almost immediately. All along the high ground, the German gunners opened up. They could hardly miss. The air armada, losing height now to allow the paras to drop, could not alter their formation. They had to stick to their course, grin and bear it. R.V. Thompson recorded: "It was a heroic, a glorious and terrible sight. I saw one Dakota in flames fail to land by inches. He was coming in perfectly when his wheels touched a telegraph wire and over he went in flames. An inch, a split second and all would have been well. They had survived the worst. They were almost home." Choked with grief, the correspondent added, "The burning bodies of those young men are one of the images that can never be washed out. We did not speak for a long time and never of that."

Alan Moorehead, the Australian correspondent, reported, "Here and there among those hundreds of planes one would be hit by ack-ack fire and it was an agonizing thing to see it break formation and start questing vainly back and forth in search of any sort of landing field and then at last plunge headlong to the ground. Within a few minutes nothing would be left but the black pillar of smoke and the unidentifiable scraps of wings, propellers and human beings." Yet another plane and its crew had, as the American pilots phrased it, "bought the farm".

Now the paras were falling out of their planes everywhere, thousands of them. Brigadier Poett, a veteran of airborne warfare, dropped with his staff into a maelstrom of hot steel and blazing tracer, "Within five minutes of jumping," he recalled later, "I had lost my Brigade Major, Signals

Officer and Administrative Officer . . . we had a hell of a lot of casualties."

Then it was the turn of the flimsy canvas and wood gliders. It had been planned to drop them at 2,500 feet so that they could reach the ground quicker. Instead the tows were released a thousand feet higher. The teenage flak gunners didn't need a second invitation. The slaughter commenced.

In some cases, laden with petrol, the gliders ignited instantly and fell flaming to the ground. One, carrying a light tank, disintegrated in mid-air shedding tank and its screaming crew members. They were all dead when they hit the earth. In a matter of minutes 10 gliders were destroyed and 300 damaged.

Staff Sergeant Victor Miller, a veteran of the terrible airborne fiasco of Sicily two years before when allied gunners shot down their own planes, sought desperately for somewhere to land his Horsa glider. Already he had seen a towplane go down in flames. Now his front was obscured by the shot-down plane's smoke. "For God's sake," he shouted to his co-pilot, "if you see a space with gliders on it we'll have a go!" Suddenly, as if by a miracle, a hole opened up in the smoke and he could see farmland below. "I couldn't believe my eyes," he reported later. "I was looking down at the very field we had been briefed to put our soldiers in!"

Miller's relief was short-lived. Suddenly he saw the field was full of German soldiers. He skimmed over a road at treetop height. One wing slammed against a pole. Its tip fell off. The Horsa shimmied crazily. Startlingly, frighteningly, they were down, skimming across a ploughed field like a waterbug over a pond. Almost immediately the Germans started pumping lead into the thin fuselage of this great lame bird.

In those same few minutes sergeant pilot "Andy" Andrews almost "bought the farm", too. Flak had seriously wounded his co-pilot and shattered most of the controls. Somehow he brought the glider down. It slammed into a ploughed field, throwing up mud and grass everywhere. At tremendous speed it careered forward. Sweating with fear and the strain, Andrews managed to avoid a group of poplars. Suddenly, to his horror, he realized he was heading straight for the wreck of another glider. "There was a bump on the left, then a lurch forward, followed by a crunching, splintering sound, as if every piece of plywood was disintegrating into matchwood."

Casualties were mounting rapidly now. Even padres were being killed. Working at a forward field dressing station, surgeon Lieutenant Colonel Watts stared around at the terrible slaughter of the gliders and thought dispassionately, "It looked rather like a fairground in the process of closing done, only the still figures of the dead gave a grim reality to the scene. Everywhere gliders were burning or tilted at impossible angles, their noses wrecked and smashed into the churned up earth." In one glider, he noted the charred bodies inside, "the whole looking for all the world as if some monster had set a birdcage afire".

The Canadians in the British 6th Airborne Division were suffering terrible casualties, too. Their CO was missing – later he was found shot hanging from a tree by his parachute. Now as the number of wounded grew and grew, a blond giant of a medic, Corporal George Topham, from northern Canada, attempted to bring in some wounded. He was shot in the nose and cheek. "Toppy refused to be evacuated," his officer recalled. "He went back out there time and time again and continued evacuating the drop zone, until he had cleared it. It wasn't until then that he finally agreed to sit down and let the doctors work on him."

But Topham's devotion to duty didn't end there. On his way back from the aid station, Topham came across a carrier which had received a direct hit. He went into action again. Corporal E. Einarson watched as the medic "jumped up on top of the carrier and literally lifted the occupants out – driver, the co-driver and the people behind and handed them down. I thought the person was absolutely out of his mind being up on top of the carrier when the thing was literally exploding, burning and popping underneath him. As I moved down the road, I looked back and saw him jump off. Then the carrier exploded."

Topham received the VC for that act of bravery, the third Canadian to receive one in the Rhineland in the last two months.

It was no different with the Americans. In that one single day, four young Americans received the Congressional Medal of Honor – most of them posthumously. Private George Peters, who won his by attacking a German gun at point-blank range and died in the attempt, was one of the 17th Airborne's parachutists. They had come down in the wrong zone, very close to that of the British 6th Airborne and came under terrific fire right from the start (in the end they would have 35 per cent casualties). Over three-quarters of the seventy-one C46 planes bringing some of them in were severely damaged. Nineteen of them didn't make it home at all.

Jumping from a flaming aircraft was a harrowing experience. "When we were hit," one parachutist, Captain Wing, recalled, "I had this wild thought: Who the hell is throwing gravel at the plane? That's what it sounded like. One boy, he got his little finger nearly severed completely. We had a bit of a flap what to do, then finally we cut his finger off, wrapped a handkerchief around it and put it in his pocket, and he went out with us. He figured – we all did – that it was safer to be on the ground."

Miller landed in a pig pen. There was total confusion everywhere. Tracer zipped back and forth. Mortar bombs were falling everywhere. By now he realized that he and most of the 17th's parachutists had come down in the British drop zone. "As I watched, a big British Horsa glider landed in the field immediately to our front and out rolled an armoured car with a 6th AB soldier standing in the machine-gun turret. He was immediately engaged by the enemy and returned the

113

fire. The armoured car burst into flames. My last impression was of the gunner enveloped in flames, but bravely firing his machine-gun."

And so it went on all day. At one stage the "Red Dorsets", as they called themselves, of the 6th Airborne, fixed bayonets and charged the enemy, an uncommon occurrence in World War Two. By the time it was over, there were only twenty left of their D Company. The fighting swept back and forth, with the Germans, especially their own paras, putting up a formidable defence. But even they knew they were not in a position to push the attackers back over the Rhine. The Allies were too strong for that.

Thus it was that Montgomery could send a "top secret, personal and eyes only" message back to London that day. In it he stated, "I can now say that the first day's operations in Plunder* have been most successful. We have got 6 divs over the Rhine, including the two airborne. We have captured 5,300 prisoners. Our total casualties are about 1,200. The bridging is proceeding very satisfactorily except on the left about Rees."

Six hours later most of Montgomery's objectives for the first day had been achieved. The ground troops had fought their way to the paras' positions and linked up. Exhausted, but happy to have survived, the PBI and the paras, Canadian, British and American, ate cold rations, swapped stories and if they were lucky had a swig of rum or looted schnapps. The paras' casualties had been horrendous, an estimated 35 per cent, but they had done the job they had been sent to do. Germany's last natural bastion had fallen. On the morrow they would be off on their way to Berlin.

Every war produces its own heroes. But it had taken three long years of black despair for Britain to produce its own military hero, Bernard Law Montgomery.

* Code-name for the operation.

114

But the bishop's son, who neither drank, smoked nor womanized was different from the elegantly uniformed, red-faced hearty general officers that the British Army usually produced at that time – men addicted to blood sports, good food, port and skirt-chasing. Even the Russian, Marshal Rokossovsky, was surprised when an envoy, sent to Montgomery's HQ to discover the latter's tastes, reported that the little Englishman didn't like cigars, wine or dancing girls. *"What the devil does he do all day?"* exploded the Russian, who had a mistress permanently installed at his own HQ.

Skinny and small – 144 pounds and 5-foot 3-inches – he didn't even dress like a traditional British general. Indeed he was decidedly careless of his appearance. Often he wore corduroy trousers and civilian shoes. Sometimes he carried his "gamp" – a battered old umbrella. He was inclined to wear the badge of some regiment, sometimes two, although this was contrary to Army regulations because he didn't belong to those regiments.

Nor did he treat his troops in the traditional manner. He dispensed with "bull" when he visited them. Instead he'd gather them round him informally to tell them "the form" – his intentions. Although he was a strict non-smoker himself, he always had scores of packets of cigarettes ready to give away to any troops he might meet on his travels. He ensured that his men had plenty of drink and women, too, if it was possible. Indeed early in the war he had nearly been fired in France because he had instituted brothels for the men of his division to lower the rate of VD.

His soldiers liked him well enough. They knew he wasn't going to throw away their lives unnecessarily. Thanks to the BBC and the popular press and his very personal style, he was known throughout the country. Whenever he made an appearance in public, the civilians mobbed him.

But it was a different matter with his fellow generals, both British and American. They told malicious stories about him in their clubs and messes. "Montgomery and Admiral Ramsay, the naval commander of the invasion fleet, are torpedoed. Ramsay pleads with Monty not to tell anyone he can't swim. Monty replies he won't tell if Ramsay doesn't reveal that Monty can't walk across the water!" When Montgomery was given command of all the land forces for the invasion, it was widely commented in London's clubland that "gentlemen are all out now; the players are in!"

At first the Americans showed respect for the "victor of El Alamein". After all, the American generals had mostly fought their last battle in France in 1918. Both Eisenhower and his senior field commander, Bradley, had never fired a shot in anger – and never would. So they deferred to the battle-experienced Monty, who had been left for dead on the battlefield in 1914. But once they got to know "that insufferable little man", as Churchill once called Monty in a moment of exasperation, they were less willing to hide their resentment and bitterness at his high-handed, arrogant manner. In July 1944, Patton was forced to wait outside Montgomery's caravan and whittle a stick until the "master" had time to see him. By Christmas 1944, Bradley was telling Eisenhower, "You must know, Ike, that I cannot serve under Montgomery. If he is put in command of all ground forces you must send me back home." By March 1945 Eisenhower felt (as he explained to author Cornelius Ryan long afterwards) "Montgomery had become so personal in his efforts to make sure the Americans, and me in particular, got no credit, that, in fact, we hardly had anything to do with the war, that I finally stopped talking to him."

Now the American generals took their revenge for all the arrogance, insults, real and imagined, and slights of the last year. On 27 March, Montgomery signalled Eisenhower that he was already issuing orders for the British Second Army and the attached US Ninth Army to drive to the Elbe – "and thence by autobahn to Berlin I hope".

Eisenhower must have hit the roof. The tone of the dispatch

was the usual arrogant Monty, as well as the latter's assumption that he was going to retain a whole US Army under command. It was the very last straw.

On the night of 28 March, Eisenhower informed Monty curtly that Bradley was going to aim for the line Erfurt-Leipzig-Dresden, thus swinging well south of Berlin "to join hands with the Russians".

On the last day of that fateful March, he added to his instructions of the 28th which had spelled out the fact that "the mission of your army group will be to protect Bradley's northern flank". He signalled to Monty: "You will note that in none of this do I mention Berlin. The place has become, as far as I am concerned, nothing but a geographical location."

Monty and the British Army had fought their last great battle of the 20th century. Now (or so it seemed) the Americans would win the final victory in the West. The British were committed to a mere, unimportant side-show.

APRIL

"Obviously not a man, woman or child in Germany ever approved of the war for a minute."

Martha Gellhorn, April 1945

I

We're the D-Day Dodgers out in Italy, always drinking vino, always on the spree. Eighth Army skivers and the Yanks. We live in Rome and laugh at tanks. For we're the D-Day Dodgers in sunny Italy.

Thus they sang cynically in April that year in Italy, the men of the British Eighth Army and those of the American Fifth Army. For they knew they belonged to forgotten armies. Everything they did was always overshadowed by the events taking place in North-West Europe. They had captured Rome on 5 June 1944. But that splendid culmination of a year-long campaign up the boot of Italy ("the soft underbelly of Europe", Churchill had called it at the outset; "tough old gut!" it had become for them) had had little impact. For the next day had been D-Day.

Ever since 3 September 1943, they had been fighting the "Teds" as they called the Germans* from one river – or mountain-line – to the other. Their casualties had been enormous. Now this ragtag army composed of fifteen different nationalities, from Brazilians to New Zealanders, waited for what was to come. Were they, "the D-Day Dodgers",** going to be thrown into action yet again? It was clear from the news that the enemy was nearly finished in Germany. Everywhere the Western Allies had crossed the Rhine and were racing

* From the Italian word for German – "*tedeschi*".
** Mary Astor, MP is alleged to have called the troops in Italy "the D-Day Dodgers". Hence the song sung to the tune of "Lili Marlene".

north, east and south-east, with two US Armies, Patton's Third and Patch's Seventh, heading for Bavaria and Austria. Why not let them do the attacking, thus cutting the German defenders of the positions in front of them off at the rear? Hadn't they done enough fighting in "sunny Italy" which had turned out the previous two winters to be freezingly cold with snow and rain falling, day after day, for weeks on end?

There were other reasons, too, why the American and British troops in Italy could have remained in their Apennine positions, though the men in the line knew nothing of them. Already back in January 1945, German officials in Switzerland had approached Allen Dulles, the head of the OSS spy organization (the forerunner of the CIA). They began the first of the talks which would lead to the surrender of German troops in Italy. By March Dulles was meeting SS General Wolff, with the approval of the head of the SS Himmler. Dulles told Wolff point-blank that the Western Allies would only agree to "unconditional surrender", as laid down by the Allied political leaders. Wolff seemed to accept that proposal without too much difficulty. By the end of March two Allied generals, one American, one British, were waiting in Switzerland in a remote villa to meet Wolff and discuss terms for the surrender of the Italian Neo-Fascist Army and the German Army in Italy.

But the subordinate Allied commanders knew nothing of these secret meetings. They felt a compulsion to commit their troops waiting in the Apennines. They were motivated by an irresistible urge to share in the final victory, when that same victory could have been won by simply standing still. So while the negotiations hung fire, the Allied generals ordered their troops into the attack. So the campaign, which had already resulted in 300,000 casualties was going to claim more now. It was going to be a last battle, that need not have been fought and which, in the end, was quite pointless.

A key role in the coming operation would be played by the

new boys in Italy, the US 10th Mountain Division. The mountaineers felt themselves an elite, and with good reason. For a goodly number of the 10th were college graduates with money who had learned to ski and climb before Pearl Harbour. As they were wont to remark, they were more elite than even the British Brigade of Guards. For in the Guards only the officers were gentlemen, while in the 10th, *both* the officers *and* the enlisted men were gentlemen.

Now, as on 14 April, the artillery thundered and the bombers came in to lay their lethal eggs on the enemy below in the Po Valley, one of the Division's regimental commanders, Colonel Tomlinson, called together his company commanders and said in a not so gentlemanly fashion: "Gentlemen, adjust your glasses. Below you see the city of Bologna, the pearl of the Po Valley. When we get there we are going to have two weeks of looting, raping and pillage. *Now let's go!*"

The Mountain Division needed no urging. Much as they liked the mountains, they lusted after the fleshpots of the plain below. Swiftly the 10th pushed forward. The Germans began to retreat. Spread out over fifty miles, they looted whatever transport they needed – mules, horses and, in one case, an ancient fire-engine.

In a letter home to his wife, one officer of the 10th tried to describe the feelings of the men as they came out of the mountains: "From the mountains to the plains a grinding job, from upland valley to rocky ridge routing the bastards out of their bastions and no goddam quarter. Then I was witness to the most exhilarating experience a soldier can have, the enemy retreating in confusion. I rolled down into the plains feeling drunk with the power of the machine that rushed forward through flat, canal-crossed wheatfields, orchards and gardens – through little villages of cheering *paisans* offering eggs, *vino*, throwing flowers, cheering, '*Bravo! Viva Libaratori! Salvi*' (saved) as they crowded around the jeep trying to touch me. Very disconcerting at 40 mph!"

*   *   *

But it wasn't all *vino, viva* and victory. The Germans, although in retreat, were making the Allies pay for every yard of ground taken. There were mines everywhere, all bridges had been blown and there were always the stay-behind snipers and machine-gunners who made the unwary pay the price for their foolishness. In particular, the New Zealand Division, heading for the River Po, was suffering cruel losses. Captain Geoffrey Cox was constantly receiving reports from the fighting troops that were unsettling, not only for him as the divisional intelligence officer, but also for his divisional commander, General Freyberg VC. One such disheartening message, which was typical, read, "We found ourselves occupying 350 yards of stop-bank with nine or ten men to one flank and three on the other. All the platoon commanders were wounded, two sergeants dead and the third wounded." Twelve men holding a front of a quarter of a mile!

As Cox commented: "Reports of this kind, coming back day after day, translated themselves into the grim arithmetic of the casualty lists, the price of our success.

"Again and again now in the General's caravan I heard the word 'casualties'. Again and again at conferences the word 'reinforcements' was mentioned."

But there were no reinforcements, save those who reported back after being sick or wounded. New Zealand, so many thousand miles away, was scraping the barrel. Freyberg knew it, too. Soon, he told himself, he'd have to ask for the Division to be taken out of the line.

But the Germans' days in Italy were numbered. Already to their rear, the Russians had entered Austria and captured Vienna. They, too, were receiving no reinforcements over the Brenner Pass into Italy. Now, not only were they being attacked by regular Allied troops, Americans, British, South African, New Zealanders and so on, but they were also being assaulted by the Italian partisans.

They fought a different kind of war – bloody, bitter,

treacherous and cruel. It was a war of ambush, kidnapping, torture. The Italian partisans, most of them communists from the great Italian cities of the north, knew they could expect no quarter from the Germans if they were captured by them. In their turn, they gave no quarter to the Germans and Mussolini's fascist militia who fought with them.

Up front one hot April day, Geoffrey Cox, the New Zealand Intelligence officer, met a bearded partisan officer with the red scarf of the communists wrapped around his neck. The partisan told Cox that there were several Germans still hiding in the area. Cox said, "Any prisoners you can get will be invaluable."

The partisan leader grinned: "*Si, si Prisionieri*", he answered.

But there were to be no prisoners. Half an hour later Cox heard shooting. The partisan leader reported they had found three *tedeschi*, one of whom had been an officer. He'd tried to escape, "*Molto stupido, molto stupido*". For now he was dead.

The partisan leader gave Cox the German captain's pay-book. It contained a picture of what looked like "the stock propaganda shot of the stern SS man", duelling scars and all. According to the pay-book, as Cox flipped through its pages, the dead man had been in the SS from the very start. He had fought in Poland, France, Russia and Italy.

"The *Hauptmann*'s book was full of photographs of storm troops and of soldiers, of sisters in white blouses and dark skirts, of a heavy-built father with close-cropped hair, of other young officers with the same relentless faces. This was the type Hitler had loosed on Europe, brave, desperate, efficient. And now he had come to his end in an Italian field, shot down by an Italian farmer's boy with a Sten gun, shot in the back as he crouched in hiding."

II

In Germany it was a crazy time, a time without precedent. The British called it "swanning"; the Americans "the rat race". Both phrases meant the armour had cut loose, unconcerned about what lay on their flanks. They barrelled down the roads of central Germany, leaving the follow-up infantry to deal with any pockets of resistance. If a town showed any signs of putting up a fight, they by-passed it so there were great patches of "outlaw country" off the main roads.

The tactic the armour used was simple, but lethal. A solitary tank or armoured car linked to the main body by radio would crawl up the enemy road "daring" any concealed German to take a pot-shot at it with an anti-tank gun or one of the German hand-held rocket launchers, the *Panzerfausts*. Soon or later the tank at point would bump into trouble – a platoon of diehard SS, a bunch of suicidal Hitler Youth kids armed with *panzerfausts*, a lone 88mm cannon using up the last of its ammunition.

Here and there on the American front, the Germans still launched counter-attacks. North of Weimar, Patton's 76th Division was attacked savagely by 2,000 Germans supported by a number of assault guns. The assault was repulsed but only after the 6th US Armored Division had been forced to launch a full-scale armoured attack. The next day, General Frederick Hahn of the German LXXXII Corps, to which the attackers had belonged, walked into an area held by a black quartermaster company and told the surprised black quartermaster's men that he wanted to surrender. Never before in the history of the US Army had a full general surrendered to

126

a QM company. The black soldiers talked about it to the end of the war.

Not far away at Regensburg, the boot was on the other foot. There, Captain Charles Long, a black, who had graduated from being a cook to be commander of the all-black 761st Tank Battalion, was captured with one of his sergeants by the Germans. Long was told the sergeant was going to be shot outside.

But the Germans were bluffing. "Soon a general appeared. He asked me: 'what are you doing in Germany, you rich Americans?'"

Long answered, "Sir, we found you in France."

The German general slapped his thigh and started laughing. Next morning the Germans abandoned Regensburg and the two black Americans found themselves free once more. Once Patton had spoken to Long's company and told them that when their grandchildren asked the men what they had done in the "big war", well, they didn't want to reply they had been "shovelling shit in Louisiana". Now Long and the rest of them could tell their grandkids that they hadn't!

But sometimes in that crazy month of April, prisoners were not treated with such consideration. In the second week of April, Patton's men finally cut off what was left of the 6th SS Mountain Division. In the confused fighting in hilly wooded country, some 2,000 SS men started to work their way round the rear of the Third Army.

During the course of the withdrawal, the SS captured a rearline US hospital, staffed with doctors and female nurses. The next morning the SS moved on, taking with them the hospital's vehicles, but leaving the staff and patients unharmed.

Unfortunately for the SS men, wild rumours started to circulate in Patton's army, in particular, in his 5th Infantry Division. It was stated that the SS had murdered the doctors and raped all the American nurses. They had to be avenged. In the end, as Patton noted in his diary, 500 SS men taken prisoner were shot in cold blood before the misunderstanding was cleared up. To be an SS man in Central Germany in that April meant you were virtually condemned to death if you were captured.

But there were humourous moments, too. Patton personally didn't think much of Eisenhower's fraternization ban. He believed that as long as one of his soldiers kept his helmet on and his elbows off the ground while making love to a German girl, it was "not fraternisation but fornication!"

Still he knew he must carry out Eisenhower's ruling. Thus it was that when he was speeding down the autobahn and saw two of his soldiers talking to some German girls, he ordered his driver to stop. In a screech of protesting rubber the jeep skidded to a stop and Patton barked, "what the so-in-so do you mean by fraternizing with those German so-and-sos?" (as Colonel Codman, his aide, recorded his boss's outburst).

One of the GIs unwound himself from his partner and said easily, "Sir, these here are two Russian ladies who have lost their way. We are trying to learn their language, sir, so as to direct them properly."

For a moment or two even Patton was at a loss for words. Then he shook his head in mock wonder and breathed "Okay, you win." He turned to his driver and snapped, "Go ahead, Mims." But once out of earshot, he shook his head again at the audacity of the unknown GI, murmuring, "That really *is* a new one."

But this "rat race" in a chaotic Germany was not all wine, women and song. On Patton's flank, Patch's Seventh Army faced increasinly stiff resistance. For the first days of April, when the Seventh had covered fifty-seven kilometres rapidly, all had been "dead-faced women and old men who glared with unfathomable bitterness or simply looked blankly while the great serpentine stream of American men and vehicles passed."

But at the German city of Aschaffeuborg, famed for its shoe factory, the rapid advance came to a sudden stop. Here the civilians, old men and boys, joined in the obstinate defence.

For six long days, the Germans under a Captain Major von Lambert held the veterans of Patch's 45th Division. As one of the GIs who took part in the fighting recalled: "there were boys of 16 and 17, thoroughly indoctrinated with the theory that it was glorious to seek death for the Fatherland". When these defenders refused to surrender, then the GIs had to allow them to achieve that "glory" by means of a swift bullet or burst of machine-gun fire.

By the second day of the battle, the Americans were inside the town and were working their way forward in bitter street fighting. As one GI who took part recalled: "House clearing always means sudden death for someone. It means kicking in a door and lobbing in a grenade and then running in to see who's still alive and who wants to surrender and who wants to die. Then it means yelling upstairs for the bastards to come down and give up. If nobody answers, it means creeping upstairs to double check, throwing in another grenade, praying like hell that there isn't another Jerry waiting with a grenade hiding in the bedroom or closet and then one house is cleared. But there's another and another."

There were indeed. Von Lambert now ordered girls and women to fill out the thinning ranks of the defenders. They hid on the roof tops and as the GIs passed, lobbed grenades at them. The men of the 45th hardened their hearts. They shot the women and girls off the roofs just as they would have done a German soldier in uniform.

A frustrated General Frederick, in command of the 45th, asked for an air strike to blast the defenders from the ruins. The fighter-bombers tried to winkle the Germans out with machine-gun fire – they daren't use bombs in case they hit their own men. It didn't work. So the fighter pilots pinpointed specific targets such as the Gestapo HQ, which US Intelligence believed was von Lambert's headquarters, too. It didn't work, either. At his HQ an angry Eisenhower contemplated ordering that any civilian bearing arms should be shot out of hand and without trial. He didn't know it, but the GIs were already doing that.

In the end, the desperate Americans who were now calling the besieged city "Monte Cassino on the Main" employed a terrible weapon against the Germans. For the first time, napalm, which hitherto had been reserved for Orientals in the Pacific, was used with horrific results.

Von Lambert started to weaken. He sent an emissary to negotiate. The Americans refused. It was either surrender or more napalm. Hours later the white flag rose above the battered castle which had been von Lambert's HQ all the time. The bitter six days' siege was over.

But the German resistance had shaken the Top Brass. The account of the siege even reached Washington, where the Secretary of State for War, Henry L. Stimson told the press: "There is a lesson with respect to this in Aschaffenburg. These Nazi fanatics used the visible threat of hangings to compel German soldiers and civilians to fight for a week." He commented that he now must warn the enemy that "their only choice is immediate surrender or the destruction of the Reich, city by city!"

But the Germans weren't listening. Resistance grew in the battered cities as the Americans pushed steadily south-east. Heilbronn held out for two days although it was defended by "kids in short pants". Crailsheim further up the road was taken without too much difficulty. But then the SS, supported by twenty-five of the new jet fighters, counter-attacked; they surrounded the town and out off all supply routes, save one. Richard Johnston of the *New York Times* was told he should get out by the commander of the US troops trapped inside the place, "Start like a bat out of hell and keep going faster."

Johnston didn't make it, nor did any supplies sent up that day. A force of fifty C47 cargo planes were assembled to bring in supplies. Just as they were about to land at Crailsheim, three jets swooped on them, cannon and machine-guns blazing. Down below the American flak opened up urgently. One of the Messerschmitts seemed to falter momentarily. Abruptly, the pilot lost control. He slammed to the ground in a great burst of flame and exploding metal. "Get that pilot's name and address!" one of the gunners chortled in great glee.

The supplies were brought in, but that night the Germans attacked with 600 men and self-propelled guns. All the following day Crailsheim was blasted by German fighter-bombers. That day a Lieutenant Max Schoenberg who had been bombed out of two command posts in the last three days told the AP correspondent: "We're sweating this out now. If they don't throw any more at us than they have done the last two nights, I think we have enough to hold them. They have been attacking in at least six company strength and they are tough SS babies."

But Seventh Army HQ thought differently. On the night of 11 April the Americans pulled out Crailsheim. The town was German again for a while.

Control had become very difficult. By now superior commanders had lost contact with many of their far-ranging subordinate commands. Previously the American soldiers had mostly lived and fought in an empty countryside, their bed for the night a hole or, at the best, a shattered barn. Now they were in the villages and German towns, surrounded by civilians who didn't want to flee or had not had the time. Here they did as they liked.

As US General Franklin Davis, then a combat major, wrote long afterwards. "There were new benefits to being victors. They were conquering enemy territory now instead of liberating the countries of the Allies. They often slept in houses, apartments, taverns, hotels, even in sumptuous villas. Once a town fell to them, their billeting parties had only to select a good spot and tell the German inhabitants '*Raus*' (Get out) and they were in."

Discipline became difficult. Many GIs violated the orders against looting. They stole and mailed back home cameras, silverware, assorted bric-a-brac. Some of the more knowing and astute sent to US addresses fortunes in easy saleable treasures, such as old masters and the like. In 1992 the German Government bought back a priceless treasure looted by a Texan officer for nine million dollars! Even today the bullion of the German *Reichsbank* is still missing. Worth perhaps billions, it was supposedly stolen by GIs in Bavaria.

But the US Army had not only problems with the enemy. The Allies, in this case the French Army in Germany, were causing trouble as well. In the same week that Nuremberg, the home of the Nazi Party's pre-war rallies, fell after a stiff fight, the Seventh Army had four divisions attacking towards Stuttgart in Swabia. This drive was supposed to be supported by Marshal de Lattre's First French Army coming up through the Black Forest. Once Stuttgart was taken, it would be taken over by the US Military Government, as it would be part of the post-war American zone of occupation.

But urged on by de Gaulle in Paris, de Lattre was driving all out for Stuttgart himself, burning and raping his way through the Black Forest; for French prestige demanded that the major city of the area should be taken by a French army.

Stuttgart, however, was not Eisenhower's only problem. Unknown to the French, they were endangering a very highly secret American project. It was the mission of the so-called Alsos Group, whose job it was to capture German scientists and material relating to the German atomic bomb. They knew that the centre of German research was located at the small town of Hechingen, fifty miles south-west of Stuttgart. It had been intention of the Alsos Group to go in with the assault on Stuttgart and then make a dash for Hechingen. Then Eisenhower had ordered that on no account should the German scientists and their research data fall into French hands. Just like his political masters, he wanted the atom bomb being prepared for the war against Japan to remain a monopoly of the Anglo-Americans.

On 19 April Eisenhower heard from his intelligence sources that de Gaulle had ordered de Lattre to take and *hold* Stuttgart, "until such time as the French occupation zone had been fixed in agreement with interested governments". A little later it was followed by the – for Eisenhower – bad news that the French had captured Stuttgart. What was the Alsos team going to do?

The thought of the French obtaining the key German information and nuclear scientists must have sent a shiver down Eisenhower's spine. He knew that Washington distrusted the French nuclear scientists intensely. They felt the leading French researchers such as Madame Joliot-Curie, were communist and would hand over the German material to the Russians on a silver platter (in fact it was Oppenheimer, the US nuclear scientist, who did that).

The Americans tried to reason with the French. But behind the scenes, there seemed near panic in Washington. Secretary of State Stimson personally agreed a plan with the head of the US Army, General Marshall. Called "Operation Harborage", it envisaged a reinforced US army corps, consisting of the 13th Airborne and 10th Armored Divisions, cutting right through the French zone of operations and taking Hechingen, whether the French liked it or not.

However, wiser heads prevailed. Under the command of Colonel Boris Pash, the Alsos team, reinforced by combat engineers from the US Seventh Army and several British specialists, set off to cross French territory, without French permission. Pash, a bold imaginative civilian-soldier, bluffed his way through the French soldiers guarding the first bridge in his path. He made a long speech to the officer in charge. He told him General Devers, commander of the Army Group to which the French First Army belonged, was very proud that the French had captured this particular bridge; and that he was sure the French would hold it against all odds. Then, while his interpreter translated the speech into French, he quietly led his team across.

A little later, the column was stopped by a French officer. Pash thought he had been rumbled. But it turned out that the Frenchman thought the Americans were heading for Sigmaringen to which General Pétain and the rest of the renegade Vichy French government had fled the previous year. Pash assured the Frenchman eloquently that he was not about to butt into their affairs. The capture of Pétain and his traitors was a matter solely for the French themselves. Pash was allowed to continue.

The miles passed. The column rolled down the dusty spring roads, through half-timbered villages which had yet to see an Allied soldier. Within sight of Hechingen, Pash stopped for a while. Here he signalled the French that they should stay out of the area for a while because soon it would be subjected to a heavy bombardment by American artillery. The ploy worked.

Thus it was that on the morning of 24 April that Colonel Pash and his men moved into Hechingen. There was a brisk small arms battle that lasted an hour before the *Wehrmacht* fled. Then the Alsos team set about finding the German scientists. They worked swiftly, knowing that the French would be arriving soon.

Under the leadership of Professor von Weizsacker, a relative of the last president of Germany, they were only too eager to change sides. Just as for Werner von Braun, the scientist, whose rockets had just finished killing some 16,000 Londoners the previous month, the land of Uncle Sam and all the goodies it could offer, in contrast to a shattered, beaten Third Reich, exerted an irresistible attraction on these German atomic scientists. They were eager to go. Thus they were spirited out of Hechingen under the noses of the unsuspecting French. Within the month they were in the United States.

Of course, they said later they had been working in the cause of pure science. They would never have offered their results to the Nazis. *Never*!

As Martha Gellhorn, the war correspondent and third wife of Ernest Hemingway, wrote bitingly in Germany that month: "No one is a Nazi. No one ever was. There may have been some Nazis in the next village, and as a matter of fact that town about twenty kilometres away was a veritable hotbed of Nazidom. To tell you the truth, confidentially, there were a lot of Communists here. We were always known as very Red. Oh, the Jews? Well, there weren't really many Jews in this neighborhood. Two maybe, maybe six. They were taken away. I had a Jew for six weeks. I had a Jew for eight weeks. I hid a Jew, he hid a Jew, all God's chillun hid Jews. We've got nothing against the Jews; we always got on well with the Jews. We have waited for the Americans for a long time. You came and liberated us. You came to befriend us. The Nazis are *Schweinehunde*. The Wehrmacht wants to give up but they do not know how. No, I have no relatives in the army. I worked on the land. I worked in a factory. That boy wasn't in the army either; he was sick. We have had enough of this government. Ah, how we have suffered! The bombs. We lived in the cellars for weeks. We refused to be driven across the Rhine when the SS came to evacuate us. Why should we go? We welcome the Americans. We do not fear them; we have no reason to fear. We have done nothing wrong; we are not Nazis."

As Martha Gellhorn summed up this refrain, which was being heard by Allied soldiers everywhere that April whenever they took a new town or village, "It should, we feel, be set to music. Then the Germans could sing this refrain and that would make it even better. They all talk like that. One asks

135

oneself how the detested Nazi government, to which no one paid allegiance, managed to carry on for five and a half years. Obviously not a man, woman or child in Germany ever approved of the war for a minute!"

III

But if the Germans in the newly conquered areas had never been Nazi, had never wanted the war, and had been waiting for years for the Allies to come along and "liberate" them, there were still plenty of Germans ready to fight – and die – elsewhere for the "hated" Nazi creed.

Montgomery had thought Eisenhower's decision not to go for Berlin "very dirty work". All the same on 9 April 1945 he wrote to Ike, stating, "It is quite clear to me what you want. I will crack along on the northern flank one hundred per cent and will do all I can to draw the enemy forces away from the main effort being made by Bradley."

Monty was as good as his word. He "cracked along" at ever increasing speed, heading north, with, at first, German resistance diminishing rapidly. That was something that his troops were grateful for. As Peter Carrington, the future British Foreign Secretary, then an officer in the Guards Armoured Division, recalled: "Everybody, including myself, was loath to indulge in unnecessary adventures when the end of hostilities and personal survival at last looked very likely."

All the same in those last six weeks of the war, Monty's armies would suffer 30,000 casualties, for as Carrington noted: (we were) "astounded at the skill, tenacity and courage of the enemy . . . their discipline was remarkable. Their soldierly instincts, their tactical training and sense were capable, right to the end, of teaching us a sharp lesson if we took liberties. They were superb fighting men."

Nearly three weeks after their defeat on the Rhine the

Germans were still counter-attacking. Since that time the British Army had been battling north, heading for the two major towns still left in German hands, Bremen and Hamburg. But the Germans still held fairly strong positions on the river line formed by the Aller and Weser. Here there were keen new formations, such as the reinforced training battalion of the 12th SS Hitler Youth, fanatics to a man, and the 2nd Marine Division, composed of ex-U boat crew and the like, who, though not well trained in infantry tactics, were fit and tough and keen.

At eleven o'clock on the night of Friday 13 April, artillery fire started to fall on several British positions on the right bank of the Aller. Almost immediately the Germans started to attack the British who had dug in for the night. Corporal Henderson of the 53rd Division's Reconnaissance Regiment recalled: "We were bedded down nicely when at about eleven o'clock we were awakened by fighting and shouting in the village to our rear. No one knew what was happening until we were informed a strong party of the enemy had attacked the infantry behind us and was holding half the village. Not so good, we thought. Then it was our turn. Whoof! Bang! Crash! They were upon us having crept up the copse from the village. Bazookas, stick grenades, a lot of shouting and general confusion all came at once. They infiltrated our forward positions and two or three even reached the edge of the farmyard, but Besas (machine-guns) got to work and we eventually drove them back."

The men of the 53rd's Welch Regiment holding the village of Rethem on the River Aller were not so fortunate. Attacked by SS and Marines, the Welshmen began to give up ground. The SS set up a 20mm quick-firing cannon. It poured a relentless hail of fire at the house held by the Welch. Men fell by the score. Some were surrounded and cut off. The attackers pressed home their advantage. It was too much for some of the young infantrymen. At this stage of the war they were not about to throw away their lives unnecessarily. They tossed away their weapons and raised their arms in surrender.

One man of the 1/5th Welch, which had lost a quarter of its strength in the action, was not prepared to go into the "bag". He was a Private Parry, who lay on the debris-littered cobbles as the jubilant young Germans searched their prisoners for the cigarettes and chocolate they craved.

According to the statement Parry made later, this is what happened: "They dragged our troops outside and set them up against the slowly burning wall and shot them with one of our Bren guns. I myself was 25 yards away and heard the screams of our men."

Later under the cover of a smokescreen Parry escaped and told his story to Intelligence, which had the news spread rapidly throughout the British Army that the SS was murdering British prisoners. The mood of the soldiers turned ugly. Later when Rethem was recaptured, a British NCO witnessed the harsh treatment being dealt out to some German prisoners by "a cocky little so-and-so" of the Field Security Police. "The warrant officer had got to one of the POWs who was about 40 and a little portly. On finding a packet of Players in his pocket he threw them on the ground and told the German to pick them. As he bent to pick them up, he kicked him in the backside. As he straightened up, he gave him the rabbit punch to make him bend down again. This treament went on four or five times."

This was too much for the tank NCO. He placed a magazine in his sten gun and bellowed at the warrant officer: "If you touch that man once more, I'll pull this trigger!"

The warrant officer ordered the NCO's arrest, but none of his men moved. Then suddenly he stopped shouting. He realized the NCO meant it.

The NCO moved in closer and said quietly to him, "I have been fighting bastards like you (meaning SS and Nazis) and unless you do your job properly, I shall treat you the same way as I would treat them and if you take it out on the prisoners because of what I have just done to you, I shall find out about it and will trace you all over Europe and kill you. I have at least three dozen witnesses to what you were doing to that POW."

The warrant officer remained silent, but as the MPs led the prisoners away the tank NCO thought he'd "never forget the look in the eyes of the Germans as they were loaded into trucks, particularly 'fatso' who had been at the receiving end."

In the end, the "massacre", it was discovered, had never taken place. The Germans had treated their prisoners correctly and some of the wounded were found in a German hospital. Why Parry concocted the story in the first place was never explained. Perhaps, as the troops said he'd "gone shell-happy".

The advance continued towards Bremen and Hamburg, but the men were becoming weary, their ranks thinner every day. As Colonel Crozier of the Manchester Regiment noted of the two brigades of the 53rd Division: They "are just played out: some battalions are less than 200 strong and they are very tired". Indeed in all of Montgomery's infantry divisions, which had landed in Normandy, there had been a complete turnover of personnel due to casualties. Virtually every battalion and company commander had been replaced twice, sometimes four times, due to death in action or wounds. Indeed, on that particular Sunday when the badly hit Welch Regiment was asked to find a detachment to mount guard on a newly captured bridge over the Aller, they simply couldn't find the men.

On the morning of 19 April, electrifying news reached the HQ of the 11th Armoured Division, advancing on the extreme right flank of the British Army towards the River Elbe. One of the divisional forward units had spotted a bridge intact across the river upstream from Hamburg at a little town called Lauenburg. "General 'Pip' Roberts, who had seen much of war, advancing from captain to general in four short years and who commanded the 11th Armoured, ordered the bridge taken. He reasoned that even with his ever diminishing number of troops, if he could get over the Lauenburg bridge and have his 'leading troops 25 miles east (of the bridge) before Eisenhower was aware of the fact', could Ike then stop the British from going on to Berlin?

Hastily a task force was rushed forward, infantry and tanks, covered by rocket-firing Typhoon fighter-bombers. They'd capture the bridge by a *coup de main*, as the Remagen bridge had been taken the previous month. By eight-thirty that morning they were in a position to start their attack. Three hours later they were within sight of the bridge across the Elbe. They were spotted. Several German flak guns on the bridge opened up at them. Momentarily they were stalled. Then the "Tiffies" went in. Rockets hissed from their wings like fiery red hornets. The infantry pressed home their attack, although the battalion had just lost three of its four company commanders the previous month.

As they moved forward over the sodden fields, an artillery duel erupted. Shells hissed back and forth across the river. One British shell penetrated the local Lauenburg folk museum and pierced the heart of a generously bewigged nobleman whose portrait graced the wall. Ironically enough the portrait was of George II of England and Hanover, who had once ruled this part of Germany.

The infantry reached the bridge. The German defenders started to retreat. Now it was only a matter of crossing. The German defence was about finished. Abruptly there was a thick asthmatic crump. The bridge shivered. A series of violet sparks ran the length of the structure followed by a violent crack. A sheet of purple flame split the darkening sky over the river. The attackers watched aghast as the bridge disintegrated before their eyes. Now there was not one single bridge standing on the length of the Elbe. "Pip" Roberts would never drive for Berlin;

Montgomery's armies were stalled in front of both Hamburg and Bremen.

"The front was so close that not only could we hear the thunder of the guns, but we could see the shellbursts in the Hamburg area", one of the inmates of Neuengamme concentration camp, just outside Hamburg, remembered after the war. But the destruction of that bridge at Lauenburg, only a few miles away from Neuengamme, meant that the concentration camp wouldn't be liberated for another two weeks. It would give the SS guards time enough to get rid of the "evidence".

First to be executed were twenty-odd Jewish children and the four men, two Dutch and two French, who looked after them. Secretly they were taken to Hamburg's "death zone", an area of the city which had been so badly bombed in the 1943 air raids that the whole ruined area had been cleared of people.

Here the SS maintained a small concentration camp for the workers used in clearing up Hamburg's ruins. Now the former school had become an extermination camp. While six Russians died in another room, the camp doctor Trzebinski told the children to take off their clothes. They were going to be given an injection against typhus. At the door the doctor chatted with an SS guard, Sergeant Frahm. He asked Frahm how the children were going to be "dealt with". The SS NCO answered the children were supposed to be hanged. Trzebinski turned pale. In his own statement at his trial, he said, "I know I could have played the hero and saved them with my pistol, but they would have died anyway, only later. Now that I knew what a terrible end faced them, I tried at least to lighten their last few hours."

So the SS Doctor gave them all a shot of morphine. Thereafter, they lay on the floor covered by their rags and fell asleep. One French boy couldn't sleep, however. Frahm took him by the arm and led him away. The doctor watched in open-mouthed amazement as, in another room, Frahm placed a noose around the neck of the half-asleep twelve-year-old and hanged him from the ceiling. "In my time in the camps," Trzebinski confessed after the war, "I have seen a lot of human misery and I am pretty hardened to suffering, but I had never seen children hanged before." Sick and trembling, the doctor went outside and gulped in the fresh night air. Inside Frahm continued with his bestial self-imposed task, dragging on the hanging children's feet with his full weight so that they died more quickly.

In the meantime truckloads of Russian prisoners were being driven into the wired-off courtyard to be executed. One truck-load seemed to know, like animals being led to the slaughter, what was going to happen to them. As the doors of the truck were opened, they jumped out with a great "*urrah!*" just as Russian infantry always shouted when attacking. They threw salt into the nearest guard's eyes and made a run for it.

Wild, confused firing broke out in the darkness. Russians dropped moaning to the schoolyard. Here and there the desperate Russians, their faces sunken and wolfish, grappled with the guards. A few managed to flee. But in the end the survivors were led away to be executed.

Dr Trzebinski threw away his cigarette and re-entered that terrible house of death. The room where he had left the Jewish children was empty, save for their bits and pieces of clothing. He tried the door of the other room where Frahm had hanged the French boy. It was locked. He found the SS man and asked him to open the door. Frahm did so. The dead lay in a neat row on the floor. All of them were naked and around each child's neck Trzebinski could see the red, scarred line left by the noose. The doctor asked for a strong cup of black coffee. Then he ordered Frahm to burn the children's clothing. That done, he and the rest of the evil murderers set off through the night back to Neuengamme. There was still a lot more work to be done before the Allies captured Hamburg.

*   *   *

143

On the other side of the River Elbe, the British were probing their way forward into the great industrial suburb of Hamburg-Harburg. In the lead were the 8th Irish Hussars of the 7th Armoured Division, the "Desert Rats", which had been fighting since 1940. The *Sunday Times* correspondent R.V. Thompson who was with them felt: "It is a difficult kind of war to explain, a very uneven war. Nothing can be taken for granted. The 8th Hussars have suffered terrible casualties and their estimate of what they are up against is a sober one. I have never known troops more touchy than they are at this moment about the descriptions of enemy resistance. They don't like this 'swanning against slight resistance' stuff because they see their friends die each day."

Attached to the Hussars, Captain Robert Maxwell M.C. felt the same. As he wrote to his French wife that day: "This last week we have been fighting or advancing continuously and we are now very close to Hamburg and the going is harder the closer we get to the darned place . . . A few hundred yards away a wood is on fire, a little way over to my left you can see our tanks and artillery knocking down another German village and so it goes on until the last Boche has been killed or has laid down his arms."

Now as the advance bogged down on the heights above the Elbe, with the Hussars losing tank after tank to the 88mm flak cannon which had once guarded Hamburg from aerial attack, Maxwell's company of the 1/5th Queens dug in at the little village of Vahrendorf, with a battalion of the Devons from the same division setting up camp in the village itself.

Now even as he wrote that letter to his wife, Maxwell was aware of a "German plane overhead and our guns are firing at it and here come some shells . . . and it is like Dante's inferno. The air is filled with all sorts of noises, whines, cracks and booms."

What the future media tycoon was listening to was the start of a German attack by a battalion-sized SS training unit. Now the attackers came filtering out of the ancient oaks of the area, firing from the hip as they came. With Hamburg on the verge of surrender and with the Führer having only a week or so to live in a Berlin surrounded by the Russians, they were still prepared to throw their lives away for "Folk, Fatherland and Führer", as the vainglorious formula of the time had it.

For several hours, heavy fighting raged in and about Vahrendorf. Everywhere the steep, cobbled village streets and sandy tracks of the area were littered with the dead and the dying. Machine-guns hammered away, grenades exploded with a crump, mortar bombs howled. And then it stopped, almost as abruptly as it started. Moments later there were angry cries in English, as the British infantry rounded up their prisoners, "Come on, yer Jerry buggers . . . over here. *Schnell . . . schnell*!"

What happened next can perhaps be explained by the discoveries of the horrors of Belsen that week and what Private Parry had said about the fate of his captured comrades. Frau Witt, who was one of the few civilians in the village, emerged from her cottage to hear yet another outburst of firing when she had just thought the battle was all over. Now as she stood there, looking puzzled and not a little frightened, a "Tommy" shouted at her and threatened her with his sten gun. Then when he saw she was just an old and inquisitive woman, he pointed to a shell hole as if that would explain what the latest burst of firing had been about.

Short-sightedly she peered into it and saw it was filled with the bodies of dead SS men. Twenty of them, Frau Witt thought she heard the "Tommy" say before she went back inside again; for she could see just how angry and excited the "Tommies" were.

Later when the few civilians still remaining in Vahrendorf were allowed out (for at first a daily 22-hour curfew had been imposed) they found forty-two dead SS men buried in a common grave, eighteen of whom were never identified.

Many of those who were identified, such as Martin Muskowitz or Josef Seyewitz, were in their teens, as young as sixteen.

Sadly the villagers dug them up and reinterred them just outside the place because no one wanted to be associated with the SS, but even to this day the village maintains the SS were prisoners, shot in cold blood by the "Tommies".

Youth was being sacrified everywhere that last week of April. On the last day of the four-day siege of Bremen, now being attacked by three British divisions, one hundred apprentices of the famed Focke-Wulf factory there were given rifles and a few rocket launchers, *Panzerfausts*, and ordered to the front. They were given the task of defending the local carriage works at Hemlingen, the home of Beck's beer. Like Foreign Legionnaires in some Hollywood B-movie, they lined up along the walls, rifles at the ready, waiting for the "adventure" of war to commence.

After a short artillery bombardment, the Jocks of the 52nd Lowland Division attacked. For the most part they were teenagers themselves, tough products of the Gorbals and the hungry thirties. Soon the Glasgow Highlanders were among the defenders, cursing and shouting, bayonets flashing, lashing out with the butts of their rifles. In a matter of minutes the apprentices broke and fled, leaving behind five boys in their blue overalls sprawled out dead and twenty badly wounded. In their first and last action the apprentices had lost 25 per cent of their number.

In that same week another young man, British this time, won his country's highest award for bravery. But the last winner of the VC in Europe in World War Two had to pay a high price for that great honour.

Irish Guardsman Eddie Charlton, the son of a Manchester butcher, was in a small patrol of four tanks under Lieutenant Quinan ordered up to occupy the little hamlet of Wistedt to the east of Bremen. A Guards patrol had already checked the place

146

and found it empty of German troops. This would be a routine assignment then.

In the manner of British soldiers everywhere, immediately they entered the southern half of the hamlet, they stopped and set about "brewing up". That was when they heard the rumble of tanks coming from further up the road. The sound didn't particularly alarm them. The officer said, "I wonder if it's the Grenadiers." Rising to his feet he raised his binoculars in the very same instant as an angry, white, whirling blob of metal, an anti-tank round, flew by so close to his head that it whipped Quinan's beret off.

They were Grenadiers all right, but *not* British! "These were the grenadiers of the German 15th Panzer Grenadier Division". Immediately all hell broke loose. In the grey drizzle which had now started to fall, the Germans came in from all sides, supported by mortar fire and the harsh crack of an assault gun.

For the British party things began to go disastrously wrong. The troop's Firefly tank, the only one of the four capable of tackling the German assault gun, stalled. Its whole electrical system had failed. Hastily Quinan ordered the crew to bale out. Eddie Charlton dismantled the tank's turret machine-gun. Another of the tanks was hit and started burning. The infantry which had come up with the tanks began to take casualties. Within an hour the defenders were down to half their original strength.

Desperately Quinan radioed for permission to withdraw. He could still get out through the fields and some woods beyond. Permission was given. In their hasty flight, they left behind the dead, wounded and Eddie Charlton. What should he do? Surrender? But Charlton had become very proud of the Irish Guards' tradition in the four years he had served with the "Micks". He refused to give up although he was alone. Instead he settled down to fight a lone battle against hopeless odds.

As the commander of the German assault group, *Leutnant*

147

von Buelow (who would also win a medal this day – the Iron Cross) noted: "One enemy machine-gun belabouring us endlessly with fire".

For ten minutes Eddie Charlton kept up his withering fire. Then a shell exploded nearby and he felt a searing pain in his left arm. It flopped to his side uselessly. He had been badly hit. Somehow or other, dripping blood all the time, Charlton struggled to a nearby fence. Here he set up the machine-gun and started once more. Yet again he was hit. Weakening rapidly he continued to load and fire with one hand. Finally he was hit a third time and could do no more. He collapsed and was found dying by the victorious Germans while in a nearby house *Leutnant* von Buelow feasted off British rations and listened to a gramophone playing a record.

The butcher's lad from Lancashire, who had despaired of ever seeing action with his beloved Guards – "already the Guards out in North Africa are adding more honour and glory to our name. Why we have been kept back so long, I don't know", he had written home in 1942 – died to the saccharine-sweet lyric of a German operetta *Im Rosengarten von Sansouci*.

But Eddie Charlton's sacrifice on that cold, wet Saturday in April 1945, would gain him the last Victoria Cross of the war in Europe. The medal would bear the simple epitaph to the bravest of the brave – "For Valour".

In Italy the end was near. The Germans and the Allies had already agreed to announce a truce on Sunday 29 April. The great port of Genoa had been taken and the Allies were not far from capturing Milan, which had already been "liberated" by Italian partisans. Venice was in the hands of the British. As for the New Zelanders, they were driving north hard. Their orders were to capture Trieste before the Yugoslavs under Tito did. For just as Montgomery in Germany had been ordered to race to the Baltic and cut off the Schleswig-Holstein peninsula before the Russians got there, in Italy, too, they were worried by the new threat that was emerging, now the Germans had been beaten – the Russians and communism!

For what had happened in Poland the previous year had shown the more perceptive Allied leaders, in particular, Churchill, that wherever the Red Army marched, it brought with it a new form of totalitarianism – communism. Throughout central Europe, it was happening, and in eastern Germany, where the Russians had already flown in a new puppet government made up of German communists in exile. Now with northern Italy, not yet taken by the Allies, firmly in the grip of the communist partisans, there were fears in London and in Washington, too, by now, that northern Italy might go the same way. Already Togliatti, the head of the Italian communist party, had ordered that Mussolini and all the ministers of the fascist state, which the dictator had set up in the north of the country after Italy's surrender in 1943, should be shot. It was obviously a prelude to a communist take-over.

So death came to the dictator, the man who had created the first fascist state in 1922 and who had become the model for Hitler and all subsequent fascist dictators, Benito Mussolini. The Allied authorities had already guessed what would happen to Mussolini – summary execution – if he fell into the hands of the communists. But the two American attempts to find him had failed. The reason was simple. The former *Duce* was already in the hands of the partisans. Now they were going to shoot him before the Americans made another attempt to discover his location.

The killer called himself Colonel Valerio, a tall heavy-set man of thirty-seven. His real name was Walter Audisio. He was a fervent communist who had fought on the republican side in the Spanish Civil War. He was a man who hated Mussolini.

Now he arrived with his bodyguard at the villa where Mussolini and his mistress, Clara Petacci, had found their final refuge. He pushed open the door of their bedroom and snapped at the *Duce*, "Hurry up, I have come to rescue you."

"Really," Mussolini said with a sardonic smile, as he looked up at the tall man in his brown coat, clutching a sub-machine-gun in his right hand. "How kind of you." Mussolini knew already that his fate was sealed.

"Are you armed?" Audisio demanded.

"No."

The partisan nodded his approval. He turned to Mussolini's mistress who still lay on the bed, her face turned to the wall. "You, too." he rapped. "Get up quickly. Hurry up."

Clara Petacci, pretty and twenty years younger than her lover, got up and started to rummage among the clothes.

"What are you looking for?" Audisio snapped angrily.

"My knickers."

"Don't worry about them. Come on, hurry up."

With two partisans clinging to the running-board, the car containing the condemned couple rolled a few hundred yards down the steep hill to the town of Azzano. Just in front of a large iron gate of one of the villas in the area, the car stopped. Audisio, acting as if he sensed danger, whispered, "I heard a noise!" He cautioned Mussolini and his mistress to be quiet, "I'm going ahead to see." He moved stealthily down the road to a sharp curve, then came back and called softly for the two of them to hide near the gate of the villa.

Mussolini was apprehensive, but he went over to the gate. Clara followed. There was an awkward silence. Abruptly Audisio cried, "By order of the general headquarters of the Volunteers for Freedom Corps, I am required to render justice to the Italian people!"

Mussolini stood motionless, but Clara shouted, "No, he mustn't die!" She threw her arms around her lover's neck.

"Move away if you don't want to die, too," Audisio cried out.

With sweat running down his thin face, Audisio aimed his machine-pistol at the ex-*Duce* and pulled the trigger. Nothing happened! He cursed and grabbed for his pistol. Again he

150

pulled the trigger and again nothing happened. The pistol had jammed. It seemed Fate didn't want Mussolini to die just yet. "Bring me your gun," Audisio ordered another partisan. The man gave him a French machine-pistol. He pointed it now at Mussolini, who faced him squarely, holding back the lapels of his jacket, "Shoot me in the chest," he said. Those were the last words Mussolini spoke. Audisio opened fire. The first bullet hit Clara who fell to the ground without a sound. Mussolini was hit too. He lay on the ground, breathing heavily. He was not yet dead. Audisio went up to him and shot him again in the chest. His body jerked violently and then lay still. It was over.

In the early morning of 29 April 1945 a removal van, having successfully passed through several American road blocks, drove up to a half-built garage in Milan's *Piazzale Loreto*. Here, nine months before, the Germans had shot fifteen Italian hostages. Now the corpses of Mussolini and his mistress, plus those of his cabinet, were tipped unceremoniously onto the cobbles. There they lay in confusion till dawn when a passer-by placed them in some kind of order, putting Mussolini's head on Clara's breasts.

A little later two young men came up. They started to kick the dead *Duce* in the face with savage fury. By the time they were finished, he was appallingly disfigured. It was the start of a morning of atavistic revenge and mob fury.

By nine a large crowd had gathered. They shouted obscenities and jumped up and down to get a better look at the dead fascists. More and more people turned up. They pushed those in the front so that they trampled on the bodies. The partisans guarding them fired over the heads of the crowd and turned a hosepipe on them.

"Who is it you want to see?" a strong-looking partisan yelled.

The crowd yelled out the name and the partisan lifted the dead man in question so that the screaming mob could see him.

"Higher," the crowd shouted. "Higher, – higher, – we can't see!"

"String them up," someone yelled the suggestion.

Ropes were brought. Swiftly they were tied around the corpses' ankles. Then they were thrown around the girders of the half-built garage. Mussolini was dragged up, feet first, so that his battered head hung six feet above the ground. His face was scarlet, mouth open and gaping. People cheered. Others spat at him. People threw filth. Men tried to urinate in his open mouth.

Clara Petacci was next. At first women screamed and there was a sudden awed silence, but not for long. Her skirt had fallen down to reveal she was naked beneath it. The mood changed. A partisan stood on a box and reached up to put her skirt between her legs. There were jeers. A man poked at her obscenely with a stick. Under the impact the woman's body, hanging from the rope, twisted and turned like a mechanical doll dancing.

Thus Mussolini's "new Romans" tormented their former leader. Twenty-three years ago, armed with an idea and not much else, he and his "blackshirts" had seized power. Today he was reviled and dead and so was Fascism. As the *Daily Telegraph* correspondent, who was there that day, remarked: "The best that can happen to Mussolini is that when a generation or so hence, Italians discuss their past, and one of them mentions him, the rest will say: 'Mussolini? I cannot recall the name.'"

Unfortunately fifty years on that long-dead correspondent would be proved wrong.

On that same Sunday, Hitler, trapped with his mistress, Eva Braun, in their Berlin bunker by the Russians, had guessed it was Himmler and his fellow SS general, Wolff, who were behind the surrender of the German troops in Italy. Now he had all his suspicions about his "*treu Heinrich*" (my loyal Heinrich) as he had once called him, confirmed.

152

Far away, on the previous day, British Foreign Secretary, Anthony Eden, had said in San Francisco, where the conference to set up the United Nations was being held, "By the way, there's one item of news from Europe that may interest you. We've heard from Stockholm that Himmler has made an offer through Bernadotte (Count Bernadotte of the Swedish Royal Family) to surrender Germany unconditionally to the Americans and ourselves. Of course, we're letting the Russians know."

Eden's manner was so typically casual that no one thought much of the announcement save a young press official, Jack Winocur, who told himself, "My God, what a story!" Later when approached by the Reuters correspondent for "something for the afternoon papers", he told him what Eden had said.

The news hit the press like a bombshell. Some newspapers brought out special editions in America with headlines such as "NAZIS OUT" and "SURRENDER". In due course, the BBC reported the Reuters' dispatch, which was immediately translated by the German official news agency, DNB, and brought to the Führer.

Hitler read the report without emotion, as if already resigned to his fate, then he dismissed the messenger. Now, however, he suspected anyone connected with Himmler. Eva Braun's brother-in-law, SS General Fegelein, had been caught attempting to desert the previous day. Now Hitler ordered him court-martialled. Within the hour he was convicted of treason and cowardice. Immediately he was taken outside and shot in the garden of the bunker.

Now Hitler realized, with the desertion of Himmler, there was no hope. In a swift ceremony he married his long-time mistress, Eva Braun, who like poor, foolish, loving Clara Petacci would die at her lover's side.

Events moved fast now, as he prepared for his death. He expelled Himmler from the Party for "negotiating with the enemy without my knowledge and against my will". As his successor, he appointed the fanatical Admiral Karl Doenitz, who had almost brought Britain down to its knees with his U-boats back in 1941–2. Doenitz, from his headquarters at Flensburg in Schleswig-Holstein, would continue the fight after Hitler's death. Thereafter, Hitler made his will.

On that Sunday afternoon Hitler made his morbid preparations for his own death. His favourite Alsatian bitch, Blondi, was poisoned. Two other dogs of his were shot. Hitler himself supplied poison capsules to his two female secretaries (they didn't take them) telling them it was a "poor parting gift". Then the news of Mussolini's death came in. Hitler's mood sank even further.

While Hitler, his eyes glazed with tears, said goodbye to some twenty secretaries and staff officers, Bormann, his grey eminence, who certainly didn't intend to die, was preparing a telegram for Doenitz, the "New Führer", ordering him to "proceed at once and mercilessly against all traitors".

Three hours later on the morning of Monday 30 April, Hitler picked up his pistol. He was alone in the ante-room of his quarters with Eva Braun. She was already dead, slumped on the couch, poisoned. Hitler put the pistol in his mouth and pulled the trigger. A muffled explosion and he pitched forward, sending a flower vase flying. The vase hit Eva's body, wetting part of her silk dress and dripping to the floor.

An hour later, as yet another Russian barrage on the beleagured city commenced, Hitler's and Eva's bodies, drenched in petrol, were burning with a steady blue flame outside the bunker. They would burn for three hours.

Once, Mussolini had written: "Hitler and I have surrendered ourselves to our illusions like a couple of lunatics. We have only one hope left – to create a myth."

As yet Hitler's newly-appointed successor, Doenitz, knew nothing of Hitler's suicide. But his appointment to the head of what was left of the Third Reich told him that something serious was afoot. He was no politician. He was a sailor and had been one all his adult life. Did Hitler then intend him to carry on the war, although it appeared to be a hopeless cause? Already he had signalled Berlin, "If fate forces me to rule the Reich as your successor, I shall carry on the war to an end worthy of the unique, heroic struggle of the German people." But he knew that it was merely the kind of bombast that Hitler would have expected of him. That is why he had sent it. But could he *really* continue the war?

Now as the British started to cross the River Elbe in force to the east of Hamburg, the overwhelming decision rested with the Admiral. Should he tamely surrender? Was that going to be the ignominious end of a *Reich*, which Hitler had once boasted would last a thousand years? Should he fight on till what was left of Germany, not already occupied by the enemy, was in ruins, too. Should the German nation, which had already suffered so grievously (Doenitz himself had lost both his son and son-in-law, killed in action), go down in flames and ashes, struggling "heroically" to the very last? If a Hitlerian myth was to be created, now it was up to the hard-eyed Admiral to do so.

MAY

"No doubt that if the piece of paper is signed, forces to be surrendered total over a million chaps. Good egg!"

Field Marshal Montgomery, 4 May, 1945

I

Now they went into their last battle, these young men (and
women too), who one day would shape Britain's future,
entertain her and determine her opinions – Captain Edward
Heath of the Royal Artillery, Captains Willie Whitelaw and
Carrington of the Guards, Lieutenants Kingsley Amis, Ian
Carmichael, Richard Todd, Lieutenant Colonel David Niven,
Captain Robert Maxwell, and even the Prime Minister's own
daughter, Mary Churchill, the future Lady Soames, now a subaltern in a mixed anti-aircaft battery, not far from Hamburg.

Important and unimportant, over the years Montgomery had
brought together all these disparate young men and women of
different interests, different backgrounds, different classes and
different personal ambitions; he had trained them and made
them into a compact, efficient fighting team. Now, whatever
their future was to bring and before their paths parted for good,
they wanted to be in on what their C-in-C liked to call "the
kill", the final destruction of Nazi Germany.

At six-thirty on the morning of 1 May Montgomery's tactical
headquarters moved for the last time to direct this last attack. It
was tactical headquarters' twenty-seventh move since leaving
England eleven months before and 1,100 miles from the beach
at Courseulles in Normandy. In that time the tiny HQ had
swollen to the size of a battalion, transported to this final
area in 200 vehicles. "We came to the Luneburg Heath,"
one staff officer noted, "on the wind-swept bluff above
Deutsche Evern, with a great view across the barren heath
to southward." They had arrived at the *Luneburger Heide*,

159

the large stretch of heathland five miles south of the town of Luneburg.

Swiftly the camp or "laager", as the staff officers called it, using the old Boer War term, took shape, with Montgomery's personal vehicles in the centre under a grove of birch trees typical of the heath. There were his sleeping caravan, complete with "liberated" chamber pot, office caravan and map lorry, all screened by an enormous camouflage net. And to their front there was a small portable flagpole from which the Union Jack was always flown. One day soon, the photo of that particular Union Jack, and the "Master" standing underneath it, would appear in newspapers all around the world.

That night when he wrote home, Montgomery didn't know that that lonely stretch of heathland on which his encampment was now set up would become historic. But he did know that the end was near. He wrote: "I think we are approaching the moment when the Germans will give up the unequal contest. They are hard pressed; they keep on fighting only because every German soldier has taken a personal oath to Hitler and so long as he is alive they must keep on fighting. Once it is known that he is dead . . . there will be a large-scale collapse."

As yet Montgomery did not know things had changed to his personal advantage. Soon the whole nature of this, his last, campaign would change. Abruptly the little Field Marshal, vain and arrogant as he was, would be in the limelight once more. His minor role as the "flank guard" to General Bradley's four American armies, would be instantly transformed into a major one. After all the back-biting, the envy, the intrigue, the detested Britisher, "that little fart Monty", would be seen to be gaining the kudos of the final victory over the Germans.

But in a way it would be a hollow victory for Britain and the British Empire. For many the victory, soon to come, would seem a new beginning. The darkness over Europe would be finished. Britain would be at peace and prosperous. But that wasn't to be.

Two days before, another Englishman who had once dreamed of the "heady New Order" spelled it out in drunken exuberance. Once he had written, "As a young man of pure British descent*, some of whose forefathers have held high positions in the British Army, I have always been desirous of devoting what little capabilities and energy I may possess to the country which I love so dearly." Now a renegade, who would soon be on the run and sought by British Security, he staggered into the underground studios of Radio Hamburg, quite drunk, to record his last broadcast.

The little man, with his nose jammed on his face at an odd angle, and with a deep scar, caused when toughs in London had used a broken bottle on him, running from right ear to mouth, was exhausted as well as drunk. Not that the technician on duty cared. The man whose message he would now record was a traitor to his own country. Soon the "Tommies" would be looking for him and he didn't want to be associated with that kind of trouble now that the British Army was just outside Hamburg. Let him drink. He needed it now.

Throughout the war, after Churchill's, the little man's voice had been the best-known to the British radio-listening public – and the most hated. For six years he had opened his treacherous broadcasts with that snarled, upper-class, "This is Jairmany calling" and then poured out his venom and scorn at the country which had nurtured him. Now William Joyce, the ex-British fascist, known to millions of British listeners as "Lord Haw-Haw" commenced his last rambling broadcast.

Most of what he said was slurred by drink and fatigue. But when he came to the end of his last broadcast, he spoke with a slow obstinate nasal dignity which had sent shivers of both fear and rage down the spines of his British listeners for so many years.

He said: "Britain's victories are barren. They leave her poor

* In fact, he was technically an American.

and they leave the people hungry. They leave her bereft of markets and the wealth she possessed six years ago. But above all they leave her with an immensely greater problem than she had then. We are hearing the end of one phase of Europe's history, but the next will be no happier. And now I ask you earnestly, can Britain survive? I am profoundly convinced without Germany's help she cannot."

Then, with one last burst of his old defiant arrogance, Joyce cried in that harsh abrasive voice of his in a drunken mixture of English and German: "Long live Germany. Heil Hitler and farewell!"

The mike went dead. The red light outside the recording studio went white. With a bored wave of his hand, the recording engineer indicated the broadcast was over; he had it in the can. Slowly the little man with his scarred face, who would prove a better prophet about the future of the British Empire in this moment of impending victory than many a professional political pundit, rose to his feet and staggered into the night. "Lord Haw-Haw" had made his last pronouncement.

The order of march of the 6th Airborne Division that sunny Tuesday morning, 1 May 1945, was suicidal but simple. The "Red Devils" marched on a brigade front down separate country roads heading for the small German town of Gadebusch some fifteen miles away. Whichever brigade reached Gadebusch first, would make the final rush for the little port of Wismar on the Baltic coast. This would seal off the Schleswig-Holstein peninsula and prevent the Russians, advancing from the east along the Baltic, from marching on up the peninsula and into Denmark. For Monty knew that what the Russians took they kept and it was reliably reported that they were now only twenty-five miles way from Wismar. Thus, unknown to anyone save Eisenhower, Montgomery and a few high-ranking staff officers, Monty's men were not only fighting the enemy, the Germans, but also their erstwhile ally, the Russians.

162

Up front marched a single section of paras. To left and right in the fields bordering the country road, usually cobbled in that part of Germany, came another two wary sections. Behind them came the rest of the brigade riding on tanks or "liberated" German vehicles, ranging from Mercedes to, in one case, a steam roller!

It was a tricky tactic – a thin arrow of under-armed infantry pushing forward deep into enemy territory packed with German soldiers, with both their flanks wide open. The Germans had armour, too. If they wished they could easily cut off the paras, whose sole armour was a battalion of light Canadian tanks. Besides, if the German Army *had* lost, there were plenty of teenage fanatics still willing to die for the Fatherland and take a few "Tommies" with them in the process.

But the paras were willing to take that risk. This was their last battle and they knew that they were leading the whole of the British Second Army. Besides, they were volunteers, used to "chancing their arm" in battles which had ranged from North Africa, Italy, Normandy, and Arnhem, to the Rhine. After all, of the fourteen battalions of the Parachute Regiment, which had been formed a mere five years before, six had been totally wiped out!

Now the prisoners started to stream in. Hands on heads, the flaps of their long grey coats trailing as they ran, bread bags bouncing on their hips, they seemed only too eager to give themselves up to the "Tommies". They knew the "Ivans", as they called the Russians, were not far off. They felt they'd be safer as prisoners of the "Tommies". That morning the gleeful paras of the 12th Battalion of the Parachute Regiment took 4,000 German soldiers prisoner. The 13th, despite that unlucky "thirteen", did even better. That morning four German generals, in full uniform, were found surrendering at battalion HQ.

Gadebusch was reached. It was packed with sullen, heavily armed German soldiers. The Red Devils ignored them. In their turn, the Germans ignored the "Tommies". At each crossroads there stood German military policemen directing the traffic. They were known as "chain dogs" by the German soldiers on account of the silver plate of their office which hung from their necks by a chain. Now, not knowing what to do exactly, the "chain dogs" waved the paras on.

The advance to Wismar continued. The small town of Muehlen-Richsen was reached. By now the 6th Airborne had run out of maps. Instead they were forced to use the Germans' own yellow-and-black road signs to guide them. But they were going in the right direction, they knew that. The air was growing cooler and there was a faint salty tang to it. The coast was twenty kilometres away.

On the left flank of the 6th Airborne's advance, the commander of the 11th Armoured Division, General "Pip" Roberts was worried. He had divided his division into two brigade groups of infantry and armour. It was a tactic the Germans had invented. Now the British were perfecting it. All the same the little general was worried he might still run into serious trouble in his drive on the Baltic port of Lübeck.

But the general worried unnecessarily. Village after village was taken with only token opposition, for it was clear that the Germans were in full retreat. Cars, heavily laden with officers and their belongings, most of the officers carrying briefcases so that they looked like clerks in uniform, honked their way angrily through fleeing civilians and weary footsloggers towing their possessions in carts, wheelbarrows, prams or anything with wheels.

Everywhere German armoured vehicles were being abandoned as their petrol ran out. Small blue fires flickered at each exit road where someone had flung a grenade in the vehicle's petrol tank. As the light started to fade that May Tuesday, the lights burning in the abandoned tanks and half-tracks looked like beacons beckoning the British to come this way.

Moelln, near a big lake, was reached and taken without a

fight. One of Roberts' officers noted as the former slaves of the Nazis and freed prisoners of war enjoyed themselves at the Germans' expense: "They had now broken about two thousand bottles and the gutters ran with wine. RAF personnel (from the POW camp) were making their way to the rear in a joyful mood and in any conveyance they could commandeer – those on carthorses seemed to be enjoying themselves most, galloping down the road." And in the midst of this drunken, happy crowd of men and women, free at last, were the field-greys slumped by the roadside looking "bewildered and glum".

A whole division, led by a general in full uniform, came in to surrender. The advance to Lübeck bogged down once more. Now the fields started to fill with surrendering German soldiers who stood there "like cattle, silent, tired and beaten". At each crossroads, there were the once feared Panther tanks, now abandoned. The German gunners, true to the tradition of the artillery that a gun should never be abandoned, stayed by their deadly 88mm cannons. But they did so with their hands in their pockets, watching the British pass with sullen disinterest. As for the SS, so the young British tank officer observed, "they were pretending to be something else and trying to slip away without any idea of where to go".

But while the advance of the 11th Armoured Division started to bog down, the British fighter-bombers, ranging far and wide over Schleswig-Holstein, had a field day. In peacetime, working men in Germany celebrated this first of May by going from inn to inn, their persons decked with "May green", coming staggering home late at night drunk and broke to angry wives. Now the Germans covered themselves in "May green" in the shape of camouflage nets and tree branches, as the Spitfires and Typhoons shot up everything that moved.

Hedge-hopping at 400 mph, with cannon and machine-guns blazing, the happy young pilots chased the civilians down the village streets, cracking windows, taking tiles off their roofs, leaving behind them chaos, fire and death. More often than not,

165

it was the crumpled body of some unfortunate civilian who had not jumped into the nearest ditch quickly enough.

But during one of the sorties of that glorious first day of May, one RAF pilot spotted a target that was a thousand times more worthwhile than the shooting up of individual civilians. Flying west of Lübeck and realising that his fuel would soon run out and he'd better return to base, he caught sight of Lübeck Bay – and it was full of shipping!

There were ships everywhere. Destroyers and U-boats, armed fishing cutters and barges and, lying some three miles out to sea, anchored and stationary, were two large liners surrounded by smaller vessels. Both of them looked as if they were well over 20,000 tons. Tempting targets. Hurriedly, as the flak started to stream into the sky towards him, he broke for base. He had important news for the RAF Intelligence officers. A tragedy was in the making.

II

The US Seventh Army, some 400 miles south of Montgomery's troops, was making steady progress, too, as it
marched and fought through Bavaria. Landsberg, where Hitler
had spent one and a half years in jail in 1923 and where he had
written *Mein Kampf*, fell without a fight.

Augsburg seemed as if it might fight. But "Iron Mike"
O'Daniels, who commanded the US 3rd Infantry Division,
which had suffered 35,000 casualties in two years of war and
which had won more Congressional Medals of Honor than any
other US outfit, wanted no more losses. He gave Augsburg an
ultimatum – surrender or be shattered. The civilians decided to
surrender. Medieval Augsburg, accordingly, did not suffer the
fate of Nuremberg.

Dachau and its infamous concentration camp was taken.
As the daily newspaper of the division which captured the
Bavarian town stated, "Dachau gives the answer to why we
fight." It certainly did.

Dachau was like a nightmare. Outside the camp there was
a kind of moat in which there lay 4,000 bodies of inmates
who had been slaughtered by machine-guns hours before the
Americans had arrived. Fifty railway cars stood there, too,
which, as one correspondent wrote, "At first glance . . . seemed
loaded with dirty clothing. Then you saw feet, heads and bony
fingers. More than half the cars were full of bodies, hundreds
of bodies.

"The best information we could get was that this was a
trainload of prisoners, mostly Poles, which had stood on the

tracks for several days and most of the prisoners had simply starved to death."

But as the correspondent reported, this didn't seem to worry the locals. "They passed the place daily and they appeared not to wonder in the least what lay behind the barbed wire. The civilians were looting an SS warehouse nearby. Children pedalled past the bodies on their bicycles and never ceased their excited chatter for a moment."

But the battle-hardened veterans of the 45th Infantry Division, who took the place, could not forget or forgive. They had not that German talent for closing their eyes to anything that might upset them. They marched to their next objective, the capital of Bavaria, Munich, with murder in their hearts.

Inside Munich that day the attempt by the German "resistance" to take over the city and surrender it to the advancing Americans without a fight, was about over. Three days before, a group calling itself "Freedom Action Bavaria", under the leadership of a German captain named Gerngross, had commenced their bid to take over the home of the Nazi Party.

Gerngross, who had studied under Professor Harold Laski, the Jewish sage of the Labour Party, had been wounded in Russia before being sent to Munich. In the year he had spent there he had made contact with a number of Munich people who were opposed to Hitler. Now that the Third Reich was falling apart, his group decided to seize the local radio station, the Munich daily paper and arrest the *Gauleiter* and two other prominent Nazis, one of whom, General von Epp had played a significant role in the rise of the Nazi Party. To aid his plan Gerngross had sent two emissaries to General Patch, commanding the US Seventh Army, asking him to stop the air raids on Munich, as the city was about to rise against the Nazis. Gerngross did not know whether Patch had got the message, but air raids certainly had ceased.

On 28 April, the "freedom fighters" started their bid for power. At first all went well. They arrested von Epp, but when they attempted to arrest the *Gauleiter* they were met by a hail of bullets and hand-grenades. Thereafter, things had gone seriously wrong. But the abortive revolt did have one good effect. It confused the civilians and military within the Bavarian capital.

Thus, as the Americans of the 3rd, 42nd and 45th Divisions advanced into the ruined city they met only scattered resistance from two battalions of SS troops. Without too much difficulty the Americans took the "holy" shrines of the Nazi Party – Hitler's HQ, the Brown House, and the *Burgerbraukeller*, the inn where on every 9 November, the anniversary of Hitler's own abortive *putsch* of 1923, the Fuhrer had addressed the Party faithful.

It was to the civilians' advantage that the resistance was so tame. For after the atrocities they had seen at Dachau, the mood of the GIs was vile. As Walter Rosenblum, an army photographer, remembered: "There was a fire fight between American and SS troops in a square. It looked as though it were a Wild West scenario. Only it was real . . . the Americans were taking a tremendous beating. But they were battle-hardened, had lost a lot of guys and were not to be trifled with. The SS troops surrendered.

"It was in the back of a courtyard. I sat down on a long bench against the wall. It was like a stage-set. They put the Germans up against the wall. I was sitting with a single-lense Eimo up near my eye. There were about three or four Americans with tommy-guns. They killed all the Germans. Shot 'em all. I filmed the whole sequence. I still wasn't battle-hardened and I thought they did the wrong thing. The Germans were quite brave. They sensed what was happening and they just stood there."

Naturally Rosenblum's film of the massacre was never printed by the US Army Signal Corps. As Rosenblum told it, "They said to me, 'this film couldn't be screened due to laboratory difficulties.'"

Years later Rosenblum could rationalize, however, "When you're killing and being killed, something happens. You lose your perspective about life and death. These are the guys who have been shooting at you and your best friends may have been killed. And those SS troops were so brazen. They acted as though nothing could hurt them."

That day Eisenhower sent a message to Patch to be read out to all the troops under his command. It read: "To every member of the Allied Expeditionary Force: The whole AEF congratulates the 7th Army on the seizure of MUNICH, the cradle of the Nazi beast."

Now there was only one more prestige objective left in the US Seventh Army's zone of operations. It was Hitler's own house, *Der Berghof*, situated high in the mountains above the resort town of Berchtesgaden. After a tremendous bombing raid in the last week of April, the great complex had been reduced to a smoking ruin. Still the generals wanted the kudos of capturing the place from which Hitler had ruled most of western Europe for so long.

But French General Leclerc, commanding the 2nd French Armoured Division attached to the Seventh Army, felt the honour of capturing the *Berghof* should be French. He set off to beat the Americans. Opposition was minimal. Gaston Eve, half-English, recalled after the war: "We kept running on, day after day. A few shots were fired at us here and there, but there was little fight left in the Germans." Emil Fray, another half-Englishman, remembers: "We pushed on very fast in competition with the Americans . . . everybody seemed to be waving white flags and nobody knew anything about Hitler."

But if the Germans offered little opposition to the French, the Americans did. Both the "screaming Eagles" (after their divisional patch) of the US 101st Airborne Division and "Iron Mike" O'Daniels' 3rd Division wanted the honour of capturing the place. "Iron Mike" ordered all the bridges over the River Saalach to be placed under guard. This river formed an effective barrier against anyone trying to reach Hitler's home. Now as his 7th Infantry Regiment rushed to capture the *Berghof* he ordered no vehicles but those from his own division should be allowed to cross the bridges.

The men of the 3rd crossed, but the French were already over. O'Daniels appealed to his corps commander. The latter said, "Just *you* block the roads and that will stop them." Now it was Leclerc's turn. He called the corps commander to protest. In reply he was told, "You aren't supposed to be there at all. You've had Paris and you've had Strasbourg, you can't expect Berchtesgaden as well."*

With the honour of France at stake, that kind of answer didn't satisfy Leclerc. He ordered his men to go all out and damn the Americans. Driving in a jeep with the General, an aide remembered, "I was racing ahead with the General . . . when on two separate occasions, American military police on traffic control tried to stop us . . . He told me to drive right through them and make them *jump*. I did – and they did!"

In the end the men of the 3rd Division captured the *Berghof*. "Iron Mike," decided he would honour the occasion with the hoisting of the Stars and Stripes above the ruin. But there was a catch. The French were holding the approach roads leading up to the heights.

"Iron Mike" fumed. A long and heated discussion took place between him and Leclerc. Finally they reached a compromise. At a joint ceremony, both the French and American flags would fly for the benefit of the newsreel cameramen photographing the ceremony. So they went ahead with the business of making speeches, saluting troops, raising flags etc. Then suddenly the French flag fell down, leaving "Old Glory" to flutter above the dead dictator's home. No one could ever satisfactorily explain the French flag falling down. Perhaps

* Leclerc's division had liberated both those French cities.

"Iron Mike" had a hand in it. If he did, he never told anybody.

Now the Seventh Army pushed into Austria and headed for the Brenner. Soon, the link-up would take place between them and the US Fifth Army coming up from Italy. For the most part the US Seventh Army was hampered more by the weather than by the enemy, though here and there the SS were still capable of fierce resistance, slogging it out to the bitter end in the wet snow and bitterly cold sleet which fell on the mountains in those first days of May.

On the coast the New Zealanders under General Freyberg, rushing to get to Trieste before the Yugoslavs, were not hampered by the weather but by the various factions warring with each other rather than with the retreating Germans. There were partisans of all races and political colouring. Serbs who supported their king in England, Croats who had aided the Germans and had fought against the Serbs. Partisans who supported Tito. Italian partisans, who were admittedly communist, but didn't like the idea of Tito's partisans taking over that part of the coast which they rightly regarded as Italian. Everything was chaos.

Freyberg brooked no delay. On the afternoon of 1 May, the British 12th Lancers, leading the New Zealanders, reached the Isonzo river, which marked the most westerly point claimed by the Yugoslavs or "Jugs", as they were known to the New Zealanders. But there were no Yugoslavs there when the Lancers reached the riverline so Freyberg ordered them across. On the afternoon of the following day the New Zealanders started to enter Trieste itself. They were welcomed by hysterical cheering Italians, a force of sullen Tito partisans and armed, defiant Germans. But they did nothing, for already their commanders were agreeing to an unconditional surrender. So the New Zealanders took over the city, where they would stay three months, living through a period of considerable tension and uncertainty which would characterize the decades-long Cold War to come in central Europe.

One day the big burly Freyberg, winner of the VC in World War One, had his first taste of communist bluster and bombast. The commander of the Yugoslav Fourth Army came to see him, probably at the instigation of Marshal Tito himself.

As Freyberg recorded it: "His attitude came as a shock. He was offensive and truculent. His opening remarks were: 'I tell you categorically to get back behind the Isonzo river. If you don't, I won't be responsible for what happens.'

"That wasn't the tone or language of a friend or ally. He greatly misunderstood our character if he thought that it would influence our actions in the slightest way. I answered with firmness, 'After that remark, General, I hold you directly responsible for what happens.'"

That week, with peace breaking out everywhere, the Royal Air Force in Italy went on alert to commence bombing Yugoslavia if a war broke out between the West and Tito's Yugoslavia.

III

It was little different on the Baltic. Major Watts, a doctor with the 6th Airborne heading for Wismar to beat the Russians there, spotted a column of *Wehrmacht* wounded hobbling towards the port. They were in a terrible condition. Blood seeped through their paper bandages – they had no cloth ones any more. Red Cross sisters helped the amputees as best they could. For two long miles this column of misery stretched back down the country road, along which the Russians would soon come.

Watts asked one of the nurses what had happened. Tearfully she explained their hospital train had run out of fuel. While they had been stalled, a band of marauding Cossacks had descended upon them. They had set about looting and sacking the train, stealing even from the dying, and shooting anyone who tried to resist. Before they had galloped away they had riddled the train, containing those of the wounded who couldn't be moved, with machine-gun fire.

Watts acted. He ordered his medical staff to select the worst cases and load them on the medical jeeps. Then he told the nurses and their charges to stay where they were. He would bring help. There was a large *Luftwaffe* hospital in Wismar. He'd try to find out if they could be accommodated there. But when he returned, he found the Germans had gone. Their fear of the Russians had been too great. Nothing was going to be allowed to slow their progress to the west and safety from the advancing Red Army.

To the rear of these frightened wretches, the German 102nd Division was carrying out a fighting retreat. The division had already gained contact with the 6th Airborne. Their emissary had been told by the Britons to hold on when he asked what the German division should do. They shouldn't surrender. They should continue to fight the Russians. Once Wismar had been taken by the British, the division could withdraw.

As Erich Mende, one day to be a senior member of the post-war German government, commented, "Now we were prisoners and under the protection of Field Marshal Montgomery. But at the same time we were soldiers of the German *Wehrmacht* who, grotesque as it may seem, were holding a 20 kilometre stretch of the front against the Russians – on the orders of a British-Canadian officer!"

By now the "Red Devils" had entered Wismar and this sealed off the Schleswig-Holstein peninsula from the Russians. Shortly after nine a group of the victors spotted two motorcycle combinations, followed by two lease-lend US scout cars, containing seven ragged soldiers and one buxom female soldier, armed with a tommy-gun. As the paras got closer, they could see the newcomers tensing over their weapons.

Suddenly they relaxed. They had recognized the British uniform. There was much shaking of hands and mutual back-slapping. Bottles of vodka were passed to and fro, amid exaggerated expressions of goodwill and friendship. Abruptly the Russians turned, as if on an unspoken command. They climbed back into their shabby rundown vehicle and returned the way they had come.

One hour later the paras, exhausted by now and not a little drunk on captured schnapps, stretched out on their bed packs in the newly-captured city. On the outskirts of Wismar, the Russians started to build a monstrous roadblock.

Later that night some twenty-odd Russian soldiers sneaked through the British positions to the hospital where Major Watts had deposited the seriously wounded Germans. They wanted women in the shape of the German nurses. A Red Devil on sentry duty told them to go away. But the Russians had spotted

175

the nurses standing next to the soldier in the window. *"Frau, komm"* they shouted drunkenly, for they had been drinking a highly potent mixture of potato schnapps and V1 fuel.

When the nurses didn't come down, they became more threatening, waving their tommy-guns and yelling, *Davoi, Frau davoi!"*

Another para told them to "bugger off" and waved his sten gun at them. A shot rang out, and another. There was the quick rattle of a sten gun. The Russians scattered. A fire-fight broke out.

It didn't last long. Speedily the officers of the 6th Airborne restored order. But by the time they had done so, there were six or seven dead Russians sprawled out on the cobbles of the square below. The first fight between the erstwhile allies had taken place. The Iron Curtain between East and West was beginning to lower.

Now the RAF fighter-bombers were returning in force to Lübeck Bay. Squadron Leader Martin Rumbold, leading the flight, spotted the liners first. Many years later he would state, "The *Cap Arcona* (the bigger of the two liners) looked very small. I thought she wouldn't displace more than 5,000 tons."

Below, the men and women in their striped pyjamas waved frantically. For *Cap Arcona* was packed with concentration camp inmates whom the SS did not want to fall into British hands. They had even removed all the ship's life-belts to prevent the prisoners from sneaking over the side and trying to swim to Lübeck, now in British hands.

Rumbold didn't know that. Now he rapped out a single command, "Peel off!" His pilots needed no urging. Their attack would have to be swift and decisive. They hadn't enough fuel to stay more than five minutes or so over the target. One after another the planes broke off and zoomed down in a steep dive. None of the pilots had had great experience with firing rockets. But Rumbold did his best. Then there it was –

the target! The *Cap Arcona* lay in his sights. "Group, fire a salvo," he commanded. At once the other pilots pressed their firing buttons.

Flying above the rest of the squadron, pilot Don Saunders could see the rockets surge down towards the stationary ship, "There were 64 of them," he reported later. "One fell into the water. The other 63 ripped into the ship. It was as if a gigantic fire ball had suddenly burst."

Down below the cheers changed to cries of fear and rage, as that monstrous salvo ripped the length of the ship. Prisoner Heinrich Mehringer, one of the few survivors, recalled afterwards, "The ship started to burn in several places straightaway. The whole ship trembled as if in an earthquake. Panic! Panic! The prisoners rushed for the gangways and exits. Everyone was shouting and pushing. But the three exits were too small. Some of the prisoners tried to fight the fires with the hoses. They pulled them from the drum. But only a few metres appeared. The remainder had been cut off."

The SS had done their work well.

Mehringer managed to fight his way onto the deck. "There were prisoners everywhere . . . their clothing already blazing. A Frenchman came up. 'All water . . . all water . . . fire', he cried. Then he dropped down dead."

Directly behind Rumbold's planes which had now broken off the action, a new flight of fighter-bombers under the command of Flight Lieutenant Hargreaves appeared. He recorded afterwards, "As soon as we reached Lübeck Bay, I saw two very big stationary ships. One was burning fiercely and the other, a passenger ship with two funnels, had a small fire." Just like Rumbold, Hargreaves didn't hesitate. He thought that these were German ships about to make a run for German-occupied Norway, perhaps carrying Doenitz's staff with them. "I ordered my section – Green – to attack."

They went in, this time to drop bombs. The attack was not a great success. Most of the section's bombs missed their targets.

They went in again. This time they hit the ships with their deadly missiles.

Hargreaves was followed by Squadron Leader Johnny Baldwin's Typhoons. They spread out and attacked the four ships below. As they attacked, Baldwin could see the crews were abandoning the ships. They had done their job well. It was time to go back to base to the traditional bacon and eggs and, if they were lucky, a good stiff glass of whisky.

Now it was every man for himself. One prisoner, Erwin Geschonneck, watched as the captain of the *Cap Arcona* carved his way through the panic-stricken mob with a large machete. He cut down anyone who got in his path. Then, with his officers and crew, he abandoned his "passengers" to their fate. He was certainly one captain who wasn't going down with his ship.

Those of the SS who hadn't already flung themselves over the side fired at the mob to keep them at bay while they escaped. Geschonneck watched as an SS man, revolver in each hand, fired to right and left until his ammunition ran out. Then the mob rushed him and trampled him to death on the deck, which was already burningly hot from the fire below.

Mehringer, who had already survived two shipwrecks, thought he'd have a chance once the *Cap Arcona* settled on the bottom. He reasoned her superstructure would still remain above the level of the bay. But now he realized the danger came from the fire and not from the sea. "Suddenly we were all ablaze. I was burning at my back and head. The roar of the flames was now drowning the piteous screams of the dying and burning. In the very last moment I saw an iron stanchion above me. With my one good arm I could just reach it and somehow with a superhuman effort, I managed to draw myself up on it."

On the stanchion Mehringer looked down and spotted his good friend, Max. Both his arms were badly burnt with the

178

charred flesh hanging down in blackstreamers. He pulled him up to safety. Then, as the terrible flames consumed those below, he and Max walked to safety. Behind them they left a terrible picture. More than 200 human beings, charred and burned, fused together in one great revolting lump.

By the time the two friends had rescued themselves more than 3,000 men and women had been burned to death on the *Cap Arcona*, most of them trapped below. Some of the prisoners had been so emaciated after months in the concentration camp at Neuengamme that they had been able to squeeze their way through the portholes. But as they had done so they had been overcome by smoke. Now they sprawled there grotesquely, the upper halves of their bodies apparently untouched, but with their bottom halves burned to a cinder.

Russian prisoner, Vassili Bukreyev, was one of those who managed to squeeze himself through a porthole. He dropped into the sea next to Geschonneck. Together they decided to swim for the shore which was clearly visible. But they changed their minds after a few minutes. For already they could hear the cracks of rifle fire and quick bursts of machine-guns. The small boats which were hurrying out to the sinking ships were coming not to rescue the survivors, but to shoot them.

Watching from the shore, a fifteen-year-old German boy, Gerhard Schnoor, could see the sinking ships quite clearly and the hundreds of heads – "a sea of heads", he called them later. He could also see the small boats and hear a German officer proclaim, "Only German soldiers are coming on board." Then he watched as the German sailors struck "at those who were clinging to the sides of the boats, striking their hands and throwing them back into the water mercilessly". But it didn't end there. As more and more of the prisoners started to cling to the boats, the sailors "shot at the people in the water. Silently those hit sank beneath the waves."

Bogdan Suchowiak, a Pole, clad only in a German Army shirt, was one of those threatened with death. Standing on the deck of a naval cutter an officer shouted through a loud hailer, "Don't take the prisoners aboard. Only SS and sailors." The Pole knew he could swim no further. He was exhausted. As he could speak fair German he decided to pretend to be one.

But his cover didn't last long. A fellow inmate of Neuengamme, a German sent to the camp for criminal reasons, recognized him. He shouted, "Hey, there are foreigners here!" The Pole and a Czech were forced onto the deck at bayonet point and kicked overboard.

Somehow he made it to the shore, telling himself, "I have triumphed. I have saved my life. Now the war is behind me, the September campaign (he had fought with the Polish Army in September 1939), my time as a prisoner of war and my 37 months in the concentration camp."

But he wasn't out of the mess yet. Suddenly, as he crouched panting on the sand, a harsh young voice commanded, "Bandit, get down or I'll shoot!" He looked up alarmed to be confronted by a group of sixteen-year olds in naval uniform who were armed to the teeth. They rounded up another fifteen unfortunates whom they beat mercilessly as they led them to a truck. Now the Pole thought they were going to be taken away to be shot, but the truck ran into machine-gun fire and they were ordered out.

To the Pole's surprise, there was an English officer standing in the middle of some German officers. Now he knew he was safe at last. He decided he would make the first speech in English he had ever made in his life. He approached the group and said hesitantly, "You have brought us freedom. We thank you."

The English officer looked down at the bedraggled forlorn Pole and barked: "Shut up!"

The "Shipping Strike" attack, as it was called, the result of a genuine mistake, was the greatest maritime disaster in the history of the sea, greater even than the loss of the *Titanic*. Of the ten thousand prisoners on board the hulks, some 7,500 were killed by the RAF attack. On the same day twenty-two other German ships, submarines, destroyers, tankers etc. were sunk, too, by the RAF. There are no records of how many men went down with them. It was a great unwanted tragedy on this day of Allied victory.*

* Every year skeletons are still washed ashore in Lübeck Bay, fifty years after the tragedy.

IV

The German surrender delegation came in a grey Mercedes. As they stepped out of the vehicle they seemed to present a perfect caricature of the Nazi officer, complete with gleaming jackboots, long belted coats that came down to their ankles, and a general air of pent-up, hard-faced defiance.

Montgomery let them wait. Finally he came out of his caravan, hands behind his back. The four Germans snapped to attention and saluted. Monty, savouring every moment of it, let them wait again until he finally returned their salute in a decidedly sloppy manner.

Now his piercing blue eyes bored into Admiral von Friedeburg, who was on the verge of tears and would be all the time he was at Monty's HQ. "Who are you?" he bellowed.

"Generaladmiral von Friedeburg, Commander-in-Chief, German Navy, sir."

Monty was cruel. He shouted back, "I have never heard of you."

He turned to the next German, a Major Friedl, who, watching Canadian, Lieutenant Colonel Warren, thought had "the cruellest face of any man I have seen", and asked the same question.

Montgomery pretended rage when the German gave his name and rank. "Major!" he snorted "How dare you bring a *major* into my Headquarters?"

Montgomery was having his revenge for Dunkirk, that was obvious. Standing next to Colonel Dawnay, Warren whispered that the "Master" was putting on a good act. Dawnay whispered, "Shut up, you son-of-a-bitch, he has been rehearsing this all his life."

Now von Friedeburg, eyes watery with tears, offered to surrender all German troops on the eastern side of the Elbe, fighting against the Russians. Monty wasn't having that. He snapped, "The armies concerned are fighting the Russians. Nothing to do with me."

While his interpreter translated his words, Monty's brain raced. He knew, if he was to get his way, he had to offer the Germans a carrot as well as the stick. He said, he would "naturally take prisoner all German soldiers who come into my area with their hands up".

Now he told the Germans what *he* wanted.

It was a lot. He wanted the surrender of all German forces in Holland, Denmark, Norway and Northern Germany. In essence, he wanted the surrender of the whole of Doenitz's command.

The delegation refused. They pleaded they needed time to concern themselves with the plight of the German civilians on the other side of the Elbe, who were threatened by the Russians.

That cut no ice with Monty. "Do you remember a little town in England called Coventry," he said frostily, "which six years ago was blown off the face of the earth by your bombers? The people who took the brunt of it were women, children and old men. Your women and children get no sympathy from me."

Now Montgomery adjourned for lunch. He took Dawnay and Warren to one side and told them to give the "Jerries" the best lunch the cooks could rustle up and as much drink as they wanted. The Germans were being set-up.

Very swiftly, a first-class meal was produced with red wine and, more importantly, a bottle of cognac. One of Montgomery's officers was quickly disguised as a mess steward. He went in and apologized for the poor meal in

German. He explained that the daily rations had not yet been brought up from the rear. The Germans were dining off the "leavings".

Surprised, one of the delegation said: "We've not eaten food like this for months!"

The disguised mess steward shot back quickly, "Our private soldiers won't touch this muck."

After much cognac, coffee and cigars, the German delegation, suitably well-oiled, were led back to the "Master's" caravan. There Monty told them that if they didn't agree to the surrender of all Doenitz's forces, "I shall go on with the war and will be delighted to do so and all your soldiers and civilians will be killed".

The last part smacked of child's talk, the way Monty said it. But it had the effect he sought. The Germans blanched. Now Monty piled on the agony. "I wonder if any of you know the battle situation on the western front?" he asked.

They shook their heads.

Monty briefed them, telling them that he had thousands of bombers available, if necessary, to take out Germany's remaining cities. Von Friedeburg, who had already broken down and sobbed over lunch, said in a low voice he hadn't the power to surrender all Doenitz's forces. But he would send two of the delegation back to Doenitz's HQ to discuss the situation.

Monty agreed and he went back to his caravan. He had played his part. Now it was up to the Germans, who really had no alternative but to surrender. But as he sat there deep in thought, Monty must have realized that his own position was in danger. If his discussions didn't meet Eisenhower's approval, because so far the Russians knew nothing of them, it could mean the the end of his career. Eisenhower was immensely powerful.

All the same, if he did pull off this totally unexpected mass surrender of the German forces in the north, nearly two million men, it would be a tremendous feat for the British Army, which had been relegated to a side show by that March decree. Mind made up, Monty started to draft the terms of surrender. The document would be brief and allow no misunderstandings.

Thereafter, he had his bath – he had a marble bath in his personal caravan – bedtime glass of warm milk, then turned in. Outside the sentries could see his lights go out promptly at 9.30. It was the time he always put his lights out on the eve of his more decisive battles.

On the following afternoon, Monty had just given a news conference to the assembled favourite war correspondents when he spotted the German Mercedes. "Ha, ha," he chortled, "he's back. He was to come back with the doings. Now we shall see what the form is. No doubt that if the piece of paper is signed, forces to be surrendered total over a million chaps. *Good egg!*" And with that schoolboy expression of another age, he was gone.

It was now six o'clock and getting dark. It was raining and cold. Overhead fighter planes wheeled and droned – just in case, now that the Germans knew where Monty's HQ was. But there would be no last minute fanatical attempts to kill the "Master". After six years of fighting the British, the Germans had had enough.

Monty prepared himself. Now he emerged from his caravan in a duffle coat, though this time he had a uniform beneath, not just a scruffy jersey as before. One hand he kept in his pocket. In the other he had "the piece of paper" on which the fate of so many millions depended. He vanished into the tent, with its simple wooden table on which a grey army blanket rested. Here the surrender would be signed.

Then the Germans came in. They saluted Monty and seated themselves. One of them took out a cigarette as if to calm his nerves. Monty shot him a stern look. He put it out swiftly.

Monty read out the terms of surrender, all the territories

which would be surrendered to "the C-in-C 21st Army Group". For it was going to be a personal triumph. The Germans were not surrendering to Eisenhower, Bradley or anyone else for that matter, *but to Field Marshal Bernard Law Montgomery*!

Finally Monty looked up. He commanded: "The German delegation will now sign. They will sign in order of seniority." For British war correspondent, R.V. Thompson, Monty's words were "like hammer-blows on an anvil, each one dropping into the minds of us all indelibly and into the minds of the Germans like pins of fire in raw wounds".

So the Germans signed with an army-issue wooden pen which Monty stated could "have been bought at any post office for twopence". Most of them were doomed. Von Friedeburg would shoot himself before the month was out. Major General Kinzel, another of the delegation, would shoot himself and his mistress soon afterwards. Major Friedl, of the cruel face, would die soon in a car accident. But now they signed and filed out. Monty beamed. He called the photographer who had snapped the Germans as they had approached the tent. "Did you get the picture – under the Union Jack?" he asked.

The photographer said he had.

"Good, good," Monty said happily. "An historic picture."

A little while later a happy Monty saw von Friedeburg for the last time in his caravan. A crestfallen Admiral von Friedeburg asked what the status of the German High Command would be now. After all they were still conducting operations against the Russians and Americans. Monty in high good humour informed the wet-eyed sailor that with effect from eight o'clock next morning, the German High Command would be his prisoners. "And I cannot allow you to conduct operations against the Russians and Americans after that time."

Von Friedeburg was in no mood for jokes. He remained glum. Later a jubilant Monty told the war correpondents, "I do not think he saw the humour of the situation."

*   *   *

While the news of the surrender, which had to be confirmed by Eisenhower in Rheims, filtered down to the fighting units, here and there the war still went on in the British zone of operations. Major Tonkin of the SAS was proceeding towards Kiel with his one hundred men when his sergeant-major spotted a large barge on the nearby canal. A fluent German speaker, Sergeant Ridler, was whistled up. He ordered the barge to stop. His answer was a burst of machine-gun fire. Angrily the SAS troopers fired back. The barge stopped and unloaded a cargo of concentration camp victims. They told the SAS that they were the fourth cargo this day. The SS who ran the barges were planning to sink them in the middle of the canal as they had done with the previous three groups. It was recorded in the unit history that "there were incidents" and "some SS guards got hurt".

In the lines of the 51st Highland Division, the "Highway decorators" were waiting to attack. They had just fought off a sharp attack by their old opponents of the 15th Panzer Grenadier Division, which they had been fighting since Africa. As Alastair Borthwick of the Seaforths phrased it: "We knew that Italy might be finished, the Elbe might be finished, central Germany might be finished, but we were simply not interested. We wanted to know about the 15th P.G."

Now as war correspondent R.V. Thompson recorded, on a self-imposed mission to find the last British unit still in contact with the enemy, they were still manning their weapons in their foxholes waiting "dourly" for the Germans to attack.

Just at that moment a crowd of shabby German soldiers started to move towards the Jocks' lines. But they didn't want to fight. They wanted to surrender. No one quite knew what to do about it. "Oh Lord," the company commander complained, "you can't really be prisoners now!"

Mostly, however, the soldiers celebrated. In Bremen, the men of the 52nd Lowland Division fired off a huge amount of ammunition much to the fear of the civilians and their comrades. It was rumoured that thirteeen men of the division disappeared that night. The Guards Armoured Division also fired a *feu de joie*. It was "Fire Plan Grand Finale", a ten-minute bombardment of an area of supposedly desolate wasteland. Only it wasn't desolate. Fortunately the Guards didn't stay long enough in the area to find out what casualties they had caused.

On the whole the strain and stress of the eleven-month long campaign had taken its toll. The reaction to the surrender was subdued. There was a sense of anti-climax. As Alastair Borthwick of the Seaforths noted that day: "Yet apart from that one spontaneous and almost unthinking celebration we never did have any keen personal realisation that for us nearly six years of abnormality were over. Perhaps we were too tired. Perhaps the abnormal had become too much our second nature. The war had just petered out and left us disillusionaed and weary, in a world in which even peace had lost its savour. There was nothing left but anti-climax."

Not far away that evening Colonel Martin Lindsay of the "Gay Gordons" of the same division took stock. His battalion had taken part in thirty-two actions during the campaign. The "butcher's bill" had been 986 casualties plus 75 officers, of whom over a quarter had been killed in action or had died of wounds. As the Colonel summed it up, "I don't believe that anybody can go through a campaign with such men as these and watch them killed one after another, and know their joyous personalities are now but blackened corpses tied up in a few feet of army blanket under the damp earth, and remain quite the same. For my part, I felt this has made a mark upon me that will never be effaced. It is as if some spring deep down inside of me has run down."

Writing about these young British soldiers that year, Australian war correspondent Alan Moorehead, who had followed their fortunes over five years and through ten different countries, felt that the youthful survivors knew that the thing "they were doing was a clear and definite good, the best they could do. And at these moments there was a surprising satisfaction, a sense of exactly and entirely filling one's life, a sense of purity, the confused adolescent dream of greatness come true . . . Not all the cynicism, not all the ugliness and fatigue in the world will take that moment away from the people who experienced it. Five years of watching war have made me personally hate and loathe war, especially the childish waste of it. But this thing – the brief ennoblement inside himself of the otherwise dreary and materialistic man – kept recurring again and again to the very end, and it refreshed and lighted the whole heroic and sordid story."

Now while the guns fell silent all along the British front, the war still continued for the American armies. Skilfully the German High Command played on Eisenhower's decision not to meet them until the final surrender had been signed at his HQ in Rheims. In the meantime Doenitz made every effort to get as many soldiers and civilians across the Elbe into what would be soon the British zone of occupation. For three more days, while Monty fumed at Eisenhower's incompetence, the Germans spun out placing a signature under the surrender terms and the war continued.

Passau was the last German city captured by Patton's Third Army. For thirty-six hours his artillery bombarded the old city, turning it into one of those "Third Army Memorials" to remind the locals that Patton had passed this way. Then as abruptly as it had started, the firing ceased, leaving behind "a silence," as one citizen recorded, "the like of which you've never heard before. Then they were there – *the Amis*!"

The Americans were the veterans of Patton's 26th Infantry Division. They infiltrated into the ruined, still smoking inner city, fearful that the SS which had defended the place might still have left snipers behind. But they'd gone, fleeing into Austria. The only German casualty that day was a deaf grammar school teacher shot when he didn't respond to an American challenge.

189

But for Frau Emma Bauer, "the first American I ever had seen in my whole life was the most beautiful and nicest person in the whole world. This man – this angel – came into our cellar where we crouched in fear and trembling, and said: *'Gruss Gott. Ihr seid frei.*'"

But the rest of the 26th Infantry were not so "angelic". They'd fought a long and hard campaign with high losses. They were in no mood to be magnanimous. Among their prisoners that day they found an SS man and a fireman who was mistaken for an SS man due to his black uniform. On the SS man there were discovered propaganda caricatures of Churchill and Roosevelt. He was forced to eat them and then both he and the civilian fireman were told to make a run for it. Both of them were shot as they did so.

A teacher remembers how first the Americans "broke down our glass door. Then they tore off my shirt and that of my brother-in-law to check if we had the tattoed blood-group marking of the SS under our arms. While doing this our wristwatches "changed ownership". Finally a lieutenant appeared who shouted "Line them up and shoot them!" The schoolmaster, however, survived to tell the tale.

Everywhere they began to turf out the owners of the houses which had survived the bombardment in one piece. They wanted the places for themselves. Anything that symbolized the Hitler regime was tossed into the streets with drunken soldiers taking potshots at busts of Hitler and wiping their bottoms with Nazi leaflets and 1,000 Reichsmark notes.

Naturally the infantry were after the local women even before the city was cleared of the last of the SS. Apprentice baker Jakob Kurz, who shortly before had fought the Americans as a sixteen-year old Hitler Youth, now decided it was up to him to save "Germany's honour", as everywhere the "frowleins" chased after the *Amis*, impatient to be raped.

* A southern German greeting. "Greet God (literally). You're free."

He collected his catapult and went into a nearby wood. Here he came across a girl copulating with a GI. "She was on top – you could see her naked bottom. I took out my catapult, loaded it with six lead pellets and aimed. At a distance of twenty metres I just couldn't miss."

But in central Europe there was still heavy fighting taking place. In that first week of May with peace in the air, the "Russian Liberation Army" under General Vlassov changed, or attempted to change sides three times in one last desperate attempt to save itself.

Three years before, the tall, bespectacled Soviet General Vlassov had been captured by the Germans at Leningrad. By then he was a disillusioned man and was prepared to work against his former Soviet masters for the Germans. Soon he became a rallying point for the million Russian POWs who were against Stalin. Over the years, former Russian POWs had fought for the Third Reich in France, Holland, Italy, Yugoslavia and, in the end, in the east against their own people.

But on the death of Hitler, Vlassov realized that his days were numbered if he fell into the hands of the Red Army. He sent representatives to both Generals Patch and Patton, asking if his troops in Austria could pass through American lines and become US POWs. Both generals said they would take the matter up with Eisenhower, and Patton, who was violently anti-communist, said he would meet Vlassov personally. But Eisenhower forbad any further contact with these Russian turncoats. It would be up to the Red Army to deal with them.

Vlassov's men now resorted to desperate measures to prevent themselves from falling into their countrymen's hands. One whole division which was fighting in the East broke off the battle against the Red Army and marched on Prague at dawn on 5 May to help the Czechs who were due to rise against the Germans that day.

When they arrived, to be greeted by cheers and flowers, fierce fighting broke out almost immediately with the remaining SS troops in the Czech capital. That day the Vlassov Russians lost 300 men. But the SS were losing heart. They were retreating, too, under pressure from the Red Army. They started to pull out, marching eastwards in the hope that the Americans would take them prisoner. They knew what their fate was going to be if they fell into the hands of the advancing Russians.

Now the Czechs asked the exile Russians to leave. The Red Army was about to make a triumphal entry into Prague. The Vlassov men were in despair. There was some talk of changing sides yet once again and marching down to Yugoslavia where a German Army of 200,000 men under Colonel-General Alexander Loehr was surrounded by Tito's men. But when Vlassov learned that Loehr had already asked one of Patton's corps commanders (and had been turned down) for permission to march his men through his lines, that option was dropped.

So the Vlassov men joined the retreating German Army, mixing with the SS they had been fighting against only very recently. But SS or renegade Russian, they were treated by the Austrians through whose country they fled as foreign invaders. They were booed and fired upon. Suddenly Austria, which had produced Hitler (he was an Austrian citizen till 1928), Kaltenbrunner, the head of the Gestapo and naturally Eichmann, the main executor of the "Final Solution", wanted nothing to do with the Germans. "Action Free Austria", as the "resistance" party called itself, was just waiting for the "liberators" to come and free them from "the Nazi yoke".

In the end Vlassov and most of his men reached the American lines. Vlassov and most of his senior commanders were allowed to pass through where they were arrested. A little time later Vlassov was told that he should report to General Patton. On the way there, his truck was stopped by Russians who had been dropped by parachute. They held up the American convoy and one present that day heard an American say, "OK boys, let it go. It's the business of the

Russians." While the Americans watched, not attempting to use their weapons, Vlassov was led away. A year later Vlassov and the generals who had commanded the "Vlassov Army" were hanged in Moscow, though for another year the Anglo-Americans continued delivering Russians and their subject peoples to Russia, actively searching for the renegades in Holland, Denmark, Austria, Germany and Italy – indeed anywhere there had been one of Vlassov's units. Thousands went to their deaths, hundreds of thousands were sent to the living death of the gulags in Siberia.

Not that that mattered much to the young men who had come to fight in Europe and now knew this 8 May 1945 that in Rheims the final surrender had been signed and it was all over at last. These young men who had gone to fight in Europe were less starry-eyed than those who had gone to fight in France a generation before. They hadn't been fooled by the patriotic slogans of the time. Hitler had been the menace. That had been their motivating force – *beat Adolf!* Well, they had beaten him.

Now for a while they had time to assess themselves as members of the nations to which they belonged. The British and the Americans, the two major western allies, had come a long way since that summer's day when their future chief, the unknown General Eisenhower, had arrived in London and first encountered that unlovely smell of boiled cabbage and Brussels sprouts, which seemed to hang permanently over his HQ at Number 20 Grosvenor Square.

These "cousins from over the sea", as Churchill liked to call them, had been the new boys then, anxious to learn, deferential, ready to pay homage to the three-year struggle which the British had already undergone. But as more and more GIs poured into the island (the GIs wisecracked it was only the barrage balloons which kept the place from sinking), American attitudes changed.

In an area little larger than the State of Colorado, two million GIs lived in relative luxury among a people who were underfed and overworked (a man's working week was usually sixty hours, followed by fire-watching, Home Guard duties etc.), stressed by the raids and the thousand scares and alarms of three years of war. Now in an off-hand sort of a way, these members of the AEF* – "After England Failed", the GIs jeered – began to look down on their "cousins".

In 1944 the Americans went into Europe, feeling pretty sure of themselves. They had the best men, the best leaders, the best equipment, the best of everything that America could produce. They had won the old war in 1918. They would win this one, too. "Hello, Lafayette – here we are for the *second* time". Soon they were fielding three divisions for every one the British could. They were "bailing England out of the mess she had gotten herself into".

The hard battles of the German frontier robbed them of some of that confidence. Losses were high and morale shaky. Whole divisions were decimated and battalions cracked and ran away. They learned that combat was not the glamorous thing that the Hollywood patriotic war movies of the time made it out to be. It was dirty and dangerous. The American Army became, as a result tougher and more professional, proud of its achievements as the leading ally. The British Army, despite Montgomery, started to slip even more into a secondary role.

The Germans, too, lost some of their overweening confidence in themselves as the best soldiers in Europe. At the beginning in Normandy, with their vast experience in Russia behind them, the Germans were the real professionals. In comparison the British, Canadians and Americans were, with a few exceptions, rank amateurs. Besides, whatever they would say to the contrary to explain their own defeat, they had the best equipment, too. The best tank, the best gun, the best machine-gun.

* American Expeditionary Force.

But as the Allies learned and became ever more professional, the Germans lost in ability. On the Rhine the Germans bungled every defensive operation and the Allies crossed successfuly. In the six weeks that followed, the Germans never seriously posed a threat to the Allied advance. In April General Horrocks' XXX Corps even found the gunners of the German Marine Division defending Bremen *facing the wrong way*! In essence, it was not Allied matériel superiority which beat the Germans, it was their own lack of morale and poor leadership. Never again could there be another *dolchstoss** legend for the Germans, as they created for themselves after World War One. In the final analysis they lost because the Allies were better soldiers.

But now it was the last time that most of them would be together with their comrades of the long campaign. "Demob" and "separation" would soon take many of them home. Many would be posted to the Far East for service against the Japanese. The British Liberation Army, which was abbreviated to "BLA", really meant "Burma Looms Ahead", the British joked.

So on this Tuesday, 8 May 1945, they celebrated one last time. This was VE Day; they prepared to go on a "wing-ding", "a bender", a real "piss-up" as the expressions of the time had it. But first there were the parades, the speeches, the radio recordings of London and New York going crazy once again.

In London King George VI told his soldiers, stuttering as badly as ever, to "remember those who will not come back. We have come to the end of our tribulations and they are not with us at the moment of our rejoicing."

His soldiers really did not need reminding. Their dead were still with them, buried in the corner of every field all the way through Germany. A wrecked tank or carrier, already rusting, with a handful of wooden crosses made from ration boxes

---

* "Stab in the Back" legend which maintained that the German Army hadn't lost the war at the front, but had been betrayed by those who had started the revolution at home.

or branches from the nearby trees, helmets hanging from the crosses at an angle. Even their vehicles still bore the marks of the fighting to remind them of what they had been through and those who hadn't made it to this day.

Captain Foley of the Royal Armoured Corps watched as his soldiers polished their tanks for the ceremonial parade. He saw that: "*Avenger* still bore the bullet marks from the first day of the Reichswald and the little splash of molten metal on the cupola flap was still shining evidence of the snipers at Le Havre. *Angler*'s tracks needed adjusting and I thought of how we battled to do this task in the Ardennes blizzard."

Now it was all over at last. There would be no more moving into the line, the guns rumbling uneasily in the distance, the horizon ahead a sinister flickering pink, the soldiers laden with gear – rifles, grenades, machine-guns, spades, packs, blankets – like pack animals, each man wrapped up in a cocoon of his own brooding apprehension. And all awaiting that first high-pitched hysterical burr of the Spandaus, which signalled the killing had commenced once again.

Some indulged in private rituals, the meaning of which was known only to them. A private of Patton's 76th Division told his buddy to stay in the foxhole they were sharing. "I have some unfinished business to attend to," he said and moved off into some bushes. There, as his buddy reported later, "he raised his MI and fired it into the air, shooting off a whole clip at nothing, at nothing at all".

Some wandered around in a kind of a daze, puzzled by the strange loud silence, now that the guns no longer rumbled. Some couldn't quite believe it. They had longed for peace for months, perhaps years, "then suddenly it was upon them all and the impact of the fact was a thing that failed to register – like the death of a loved one," so the historian of the US 3rd Division wrote, "like some involved bit of philosophical reasoning(it) had to be taken in again and again in small doses. The sure knowledge of the fact was there, but the full implication of it needed much time and serious consideration."

Engineer Sgt Giles, serving with Patton in Austria, wrote to his wife that day, "The war is over! All we can think about is thank God, thank God! I'm sure everybody thought what I did. I made it. I made it all the way. Nobody is going to shoot at me any more. I can't be killed. *I have made it!* Yet there is a queer kind of letdown. We have waited for this day so long. We don't yet believe it. My reaction has been a feeling of terrible weariness and then weakness and then sleepiness. But I *am* happy. So *damned happy!* It's over."

Most of them would absorb the fact that the war was over in time, but there would be those who would never rid themselves of the great conflict. In the years to come there would be odd moments when they would become pensive, sulky, cut off, knowing that the civilians had never understood what they had been through "over there".

As writer Paul Russell, who had been wounded as an officer in the US infantry, wrote many years later: (The veterans) "were of the conviction that optimistic publicity and euphemism had rendered their experience so falsely that it would never be readily communicable . . . what had happened to them had been sanitized and Norman Rockwellized not to mention Disneyfied".

Some, a few, would bear the war with them for every hour of their remaining lives until the day they died. Audie Murphy, the future movie star and war hero, on leave in Cannes, already sensed he was cut off. He went out into the streets crowded with cheering merrymakers. "I feel only a vague irritation. I want company and I want to be alone. I want to talk and I want to be silent. I want to sit and I want to walk. There is VE Day without, but no peace within."

And there never would be any peace for Audie Murphy. He would sleep with a loaded .45 under his pillow and without lights, plagued by dreams of battle to the very end.

Some simply got blind-drunk.

It was Tuesday, 8 May 1945 – Victory in Europe Day. It was all over.

ENVOI

"Life to be sure, is nothing much to lose,
But young men think it is and we were young . . ."

A.E. Housman.

The Germans called it *die Stunde Null.**

It was a time without precedent, a chaos without parallel. One of the world's most prosperous, civilized countries had broken down almost completely. In most places there was no gas, no electricity, no running water and precious little food. There was no public transport, no mail. The telephones didn't work and single sheet newspapers in German were published only in the border areas which had been conquered by the victorious allies months before. Most Germans without a radio might have been living on the moon and not in central Europe; for news of what was happening outside their country was a precious rarity.

Over three-and-a-half-million Germans had been killed in the *Wehrmacht*. Half-a-million civilians had perished in the bombing, which had destroyed fifty-three major cities up to seventy per cent. There were two million cripples in the country. Currently one-and-a-half million Germans were fleeing from the East into what would become West Germany. In addition, there were ten million displaced persons from a dozen different European countries, released from their camps and places of employment. They wandered the roads of the former Third Reich trying to reach their homelands. Others, especially those from the new Soviet bloc, who didn't want to return to their native countries, lived off their wits. They looted, stole, murdered, raped, marauding in armed bands from camps

* Literally "the zero hour", ie. nadir.

201

in the forests, trying to make up their minds what to do next before the occupying powers' troops caught up with them.

David Niven, the Hollywood star by now Lieutenant Colonel Niven, making his way through "liberated workers" wandering "dazedly all over the place" came across a little group with farm sacks thrown over their backs against the bitter rain. They were led by an elderly man. As Niven recalled long afterwards: "I had never seen such utter weariness, such blank despair on a human face before." The German – for he turned out to be a German – told Niven he was a general trying to escape west. Niven nodded his understanding and then noting that despite the ragged civilian clothing, the general was still wearing his *Wehrmacht* boots, said "Go ahead, sir," adding sharply, "but please cover up those bloody boots."

That little encounter that May between the product of Tinseltown and the elderly German general was typical. Millions of all races and classes were on the move. There were even Koreans, whose language no one understood. They had fought in the Japanese Army in the 30s (Korea had been a Japanese colony then), been captured by the Russians, had gone over to the Germans once they had been captured by the *Wehrmacht* and were now heading east in a vain attempt to reach their homeland.

For the great majority of Germans, especially those living in the shattered cities, life was a matter of squalor and hunger. Some had fashioned themselves caves in the ruins, where they eked out a miserable existence hauling water from wells and cooking over fires of branches and planks as if they were back in the Stone Age. Others lived like apes high up in bombed-out apartments, reaching their crude perches by ropes or planks balanced precariously from one wrecked floor to another. In the ruined West Germany of May 1945 ten people lived where once six had done so.

The black market thrived naturally. The supply system had broken down and the mark was worthless. On the whole till

1944 Germany had had a good war as far as food was concerned. There had been none of the British "one egg per person per week *per-haps*!" Even that staple of the British working class in the Depression, fish and chips, had been hit because there had been no fish. Now in this month of defeat, the Germans started to learn what starvation was. The German fat ration was two ounces, meat three and a half, fish limited to three ounces. Bread, the great staple of the German diet, was cut to two pounds per person per week. Indeed by the end of the year, as Montgomery himself would point out, the Germans would be existing on half the calories given to the poor wretches in Belsen concentration camp.

So it was that the Germans turned to the black market for their survival. And the black market was, in essence, the Allied soldier with his cans of food, cigarettes, chocolate and the like. Now family heirlooms went, and family honour as well.

"Dont get chummy with Jerry," the *Stars and Stripes* exhorted its readers. "In heart, body and spirit, every German is Hitler." The troops took little notice. There were fortunes to be made out there on the ruined streets for the big-time operators and, as for the ordinary GI, as long as he had the "goodies", he could have any woman he fancied. To the victor belonged the spoils.

There were consequences naturally. In the six months from May to December 1945, twenty to thirty thousand illegitimate children were born to German women, with American fathers. In Germany as a whole illegitimate births rose by 10 per cent in that same period. Today there are thousands and thousands of elderly Germans whose fathers were British, American, Canadian, French, Russian and so on.

Venereal disease spread like some medieval plague. In Frankfurt, Eisenhower's new HQ, for example, the syphilis rate went up a staggering 200 per cent on the 1939 figure. It was no different in the biggest city in the British Zone of Occupation – Hamburg.

By the summer of 1945 a secret British Army Medical Corps report estimated that one in every eight British soldiers would succumb to VD by the end of the year. Desperately the authorities attempted to fight the scourge. They organized surprise street raids. Whole areas, usually around canteens and railway stations, were cordoned off and any woman apprehended there was taken away to be examined for VD.

Any woman between the ages of 16 and 60, whether she was a hardened whore or a virginal schoolgirl was hauled away in open trucks to be checked at the nearest clinc. But even if the woman were found to be suffering from the disease there was little the harassed German doctors could do. They had no pencillin like the Allied authorities.

"In this economic set-up," one secret Allied survey reported that year, "sex relations, which function like any other commodity, assume a very low value . . . the average young man in the occupation army is afforded an unparalleled opportunity for sexual exposure." As the cynical young British soldiers quipped, "A tin of corned beef means eternal true love."

This then was the Germany that the victors left behind them when, in due course, they returned to civilian life in their own countries or, for regular soldiers, new wars in Africa and Asia. It was a ruined country, living a sub-marginal existence, its morale and morality shattered. Many thought that Germany would never again achieve the status of even a third-rate power. But they were mistaken, those young conquerors with their combat infantryman's badge, France and Germany stars, Victory medals and all the other bits of brass and copper which their grateful governments had heaped upon them.

Ten years later the roles, as far as Britain and Germany were concerned at least, had been reversed. By then Germay was experiencing its economic miracle and was flush with the "hard" D-Mark. On the other hand, Britain, the victor, had just got rid of rationing, the pound sterling was weak and the country was fighting another of that succession of colonial wars that she would continue to fight until finally the "Empire upon which the sun never sets" was taken away from her.

Almost fifty years later, thanks to the protection of Nato and, in particular, to that "forgotten American army", the US Seventh Army, which had spent nearly half a century in Germany, the communist threat had been beaten, the Cold War was over and Germany had been reunited. Today, a nation of 80,000,000 people, it is Europe's strongest power. In 1995, fifty years after its terrible defeat that spring, a reunited Germany dominates European affairs. Once more it is, ironically enough, "Germany's century".

On 5 May 1945 after the Germans and Montgomery had signed the surrender document at *Luneburger Heide*, an oak plaque was erected on the spot where the tent in which the surrender document was presented to a tearful Admiral von Friedeburg, had stood. Then the site was renamed "Victory Hill". Three days later the plaque was stolen. Another replaced it and in the following September it, too, was removed by persons unknown and found some 400 yards away, daubed with paint.

The authorities decided that the wooden marker, which could be stolen so easily had to go. In November 1945 it was replaced by a stone marker, weighing nine tons. A little later a guardroom was erected nearby and five Germans were employed to guard the memorial at a wage of eighty-nine pfennigs an hour, the equivalent then of ten pence.

All went well for over a decade, especially as the British authorities made the local burgomaster responsible for the security of the stone. But in 1958 the area in which it stood was designated to become a battle school for the newly-formed West German Army, the *Bundeswehr*. It was decided that the monument would have to go. Montgomery was consulted. He decided it should be removed to the safety of Sandhurst. This was done and the monument was re-erected on New College Square, opposite the officers' mess. In his re-inaugural speech

205

of 29 November, 1958, Montgomery explained why he had selected Sandhurst. He said: "The stone commemorates the climax of over five years of hard fighting at sea, in the air and on the land . . . It now stands where what it says can reach the right men, the future officers of the armed forces of Britain. They are the right men because the key to all that happened was leadership."

Thus in Germany "Victory Hill" disappeared and the site of the great victory of 1945 reverted to its original German name – Timeloberg. Today half a century later all that remains of Germany's surrender on that historic, rain-swept May afternoon are the two concrete supports of the long vanished memorial on "Victory Hill". Understandably, the Germans have always wanted to forget their past.

It is pretty much the same everywhere in Germany where the last battles took place. There is little tangible evidence of all that tremendous effort, those scenes of desperate action, where young men, British, American, Canadian and German fought, suffered and died by their thousand. The fields and low hills once littered by the ghastly debris of war, shattered tanks, abandoned guns, still figures in khaki and grey, have long reverted to their former state. The black German names on the yellow road signs, which once meant horror and terror – the sudden blast of an 88mm cannon, the blue angry flame of a flame-thrower, the obscene howl of a mutiple mortar, "the moaning Minnie" – are once again just indications of the way to go. No longer has the path forward got to be bought with young men's lives.

Here and there one can catch a glimpse of that long-forgotten time: the woods on the German border where they fought that January-February are full of water-logged foxholes and the shattered bunkers of the Siegfried line; the villages around the Rhine, where back in March 1945 Churchill had wished his soldiers to go into battle wearing red coats, and where today the older red-brick farmhouses still bear the rough scars of German shell bursts; a handful of wooden huts which once housed thousands of British naval prisoners at Wesertimke just round the corner from where that proud "Mick", Irish Guardsman Eddie Charlton, won the last VC of the war in Europe and paid for it with his life. As always – and rightly so – time and nature have drawn a green cloak over the bloody scenes of that terrible time.

The cemeteries are there, of course. Unlike the victorious American Army, which would not allow its dead to be buried in Germany, the British Army left its dead where they fell. For the most part the cemeteries harbour the bodies of Montgomery's teenage replacements, who made up his infantry divisions in the end, boys of eighteen and nineteen killed in the moment of victory, dead before they had begun to live.

But these are not Kipling's "silent cities" of the Great War, huge sprawling acres of white crosses, nor the great cemeteries of the Western Desert, such as the one at El Alamein. "I couldn't sleep last night," Montgomery confessed on his death bed. "I can't have long to go now. I've got to meet God and explain all those men I killed at El Alamein." These war cemeteries near Munster, Celle and the like in north Germany, are small, quiet, reflective places.

But the dying Field Marshal need not have been so troubled that he had led these young men to their deaths. At the zenith of the British Empire they had achieved the high hopes he had set for them. With the odds stacked against them – and him – after the defeat of Dunkirk, they had rallied and finally vindicated the British ethos. Together with their American and Canadian comrades they had vanquished the cruel and unworthy.

Ending his account of the activities of his battalion of the King's Own Scottish Borderers in the 1944–45 campaign, ex-Captain Robert Woollcombe wrote: "Some remain in the Fields they won; the others, I suppose, are ordinary human beings again."

207

But were – are – they? Could they ever forget what it was like? Going up in the rain, jerkins and coats slick and gleaming, shoulders bent under their load, faces strained and serious, with the lowering sound of the guns behind them, passing the waiting ambulances, their drivers smoking and pretending not to see them, but seeing them all the same. The sudden clatter of machine-guns like someone running a stick along a length of iron railing.

Then some of them would come back. Running perhaps, shouting, eyes wild and with unreasoning fear, or hobbling or hopping, one arm outstretched like a blind man feeling his way, or slung over the front of a muddy jeep, with the ugly yellow shell dressing clamped over their wounds already turning scarlet; or doubling back with terrified prisoners, red with fury, cursing and threatening, prodding the POWs with their bayonets when they seemed to be slowing down. *"Mak schnell, you Jerry buggers . . . mak schnell!"*

The still khaki-clad bodies in the cratered fields, all boots, forlorn and abandoned, the price of victory. Their comrades plodding on to their inevitable fate, a few cocky with helmets tilted rakishly, fag ends stuck behind their ears. But most of them sombre, intent, *knowing*, grey ghosts vanishing into the brown drifting smoke of the time, boots soundless, the thunder of the guns muted, the cries of rage, surprise, pain, triumph softened almost gone now, echoing down the long tunnel of time, Germans, Americans, Canadians, Britons, friend and foe alike, united in death or memory.

Ordinary human beings?

No, just the Poor Bloody Infantry . . .

Bibliography

Atwell, Lester: *Private*, Dell, New York, 1946

Barclay C.: *The History of the 53rd Welsh Division in WWII*, W. Clowes, London, 1956

Clostermann P.: *The Big Show*, Corgi, London, 1952

Codman C.: *Drive*, Little Brown, Boston, 1957

Corrigan K.: *The Last Full Measure*, Atlantic Monthly, 1946

Dunlop J.: *The Capitulation of Hamburg*, Journal of the Royal Institute

Edited: *The Seventh United States Army in France and Germany 1944/45*, Heidelberg, 1945

Erskine D.: *The Scots Guards*, W. Clowes, London, 1956

Foley J.: *Mailed Fist*, Panther, 1955

Gavin J.: *On To Berlin*, Bantam, New York, 1978

Giles, James: *The GI Journals of Sgt Giles*, Houghton Mifflin, Boston, 1953

Horbe A. and Montgomery D.: *The Lonely Leader*, Macmillan, London, 1994

Huie W.: *The Execution of Private Slovak*, Panther, London, 1956

Irving D.: *The War Between the Generals*, A. Lane, London, 1981

Murphy A.: *To Hell and Back*, Corgi, London, 1950

Moorehead, Alan: *Eclipse*, Hamish Hamilton, 1946

Peters R.: *Zwölf Jahre Bremen*, Bremen, 1951

Pence D. and Petersen H.: *Ordeal in the Vosges*, Transition Press, Stanford, 1981

Russell J.: *No Triumphant Procession*, Arms and Armour, London, 1994

Scott H.: *The Blue and White Devils*, Battery Press, Nashville, 1980

Thompson R.: *Men Under Fire*, MacDonald, London, 1953

Toland J.: *The Last 100 Days*, Random House, 1978

Woehlkens E.: *Uelzen in den letzten Kriegstagen*, Uelzen, 1970